MW00948076

t.A.T.u.
story

Reconstruction of the rise and fall of the most controversial pop duo of the 2000s

Alessandro Paolinelli

Translation by Kay Hamdan

Copyright © 2014 Alessandro Paolinelli

All rights reserved.

ISBN: 1497327385

ISBN-13: 978-1497327382

For my wife Alessandra

CONTENTS

ACKNOWLEDGEMENTS

It's been a little over a year between that first conversation with Sven Martin in the summer when I first got the idea for this book and finally completing the manuscript. Within this essentially short space of time some surprising things came up right at the moment I was setting pen to paper to write the first lines: in addition to the invaluable access I had to key players in the story, amongst whom Sergio Galoyan figures very highly for giving generously of his time, enabling me to gain insights into the artistic life of t.A.T.u., I also had the opportunity to participate personally in Lena Katina's solo career, in the guise of executive producer for the video of her second single, *Lift Me Up*. I must also express my gratitude once more to my friend Sven, and of course to Lena Katina, for the opportunity to observe at closer quarters than a mere consumer the intricacies of modern pop music production. I'm also deeply grateful to Lena Katina for the time she spent with me, retracing the twelve years of her life in t.A.T.u.

Finally, a big thank you to Irina Agafonova for translating documents and for her assistance with contacting Vitaly Mansky and Elena Kiper in Russian.

FOREWORD

Popular and mass culture is not an easy subject to tackle. It has a great deal of influence on our lives and the way we view the world, and many attempts have been made over the years to approach it with some degree of scientific rigour, but in spite of this any attempt to take The Beatles, or Madonna, or Lady Gaga as the subject of a piece of writing still tends to be dismissed by Italian academia as a waste of time. Apart from the occasional TV and newspaper article, discussion of them is relegated to the pages of the ever-dwindling and internet-stifled specialist press, and in reverential tones that are rarely allowed to go beyond the hagiography typical of teenage magazines.

Fortunately this is not the case in the United States and the English-speaking world in general where mass culture is now fully accepted as one of the strands in their *cultural studies*, long-established university presses there have now been devoting space to literary essays on phenomena of popular culture for some time.

Harvard University Press, for example, as far back as 1989 published the monumental *Lipstick Traces: A Secret History of the Twentieth Century* by Greil Marcus, journalist and essayist, and author also of *Mystery Train:* an extraordinary history of America as seen through its popular music. *Lipstick* used the movements of the Sex Pistols at their final concert to discuss the links between rock music and cutting-edge artists of the twentieth century, the culture industry in general and the influence that all this has had on our lives.

But in Italy writing about pop music has always been restricted and is often confined to amateur spheres; it's a long way from achieving academic recognition. Even today, the various artists are rarely mentioned in terms that go beyond a basic, indifferently-composed biography; the creative, poetic and commercial qualities that determine an artist's success or failure are almost never explored. Interviews with any artist, big or small, often focus on shallow trivia - in the questions they're asked and consequently in the replies they're obliged to give - and reviews of albums and concerts often contain little more than the record label's promotional press release.

So basically it's a question of method: how can you talk about an artist or a record or a concert without it becoming a tedious report or a gushing tribute to the artist or event in question?

Alessandro Paolinelli's exposé of the Russian pop phenomenon t.A.T.u, who rocketed to international fame and drew attention to a market for the music industry hitherto unknown outside the confines of the Russin Federation, is a useful contribution in the search for an answer.

Driven solely by passion for his subject, the author has reconstructed the story of Lena Katina and Julia Volkova and the creativity, the commercialism, the publicity and the improvisation that steered them to worldwide fame, albeit for only a short time.

This is not a defense of the two girls and their music, it's an alternative view substantiated by interviews, articles, blogs and much unpublished material that provides a foundation for the work to be established as an authentic history and analysis of this pop phenomenon, independent of the girls themselves and of their managers and producers. It shows how chance circumstances can lead to success, how a pop phenomenon was created not as a project by some shrewd producer in Los Angeles or London, but through the intuition of people who, almost naively, recognised the talent of these two girls and the chemistry between them.

The thing I find most striking about this book; a book written not because there's a ready market for it in Italy since hardly anyone in Italy even remembers t.A.T.u., but for the simple reason that when you believe in something and fall in love with a story, you follow it through right to the end; it's the rigour with which Paolinelli has approached a subject area that's never been tackled before, and the pleasing professionalism with which he dissects this story of Russian pop. At the end of it we emerge not just with a deeper understanding of Lena and Julia's journey, but more importantly, with the impression that popular music and its protagonists can be written about from a different perspective; one that doesn't alienate readers but inspires them with a thoughtful biography untainted by needless fan worship. It's a biography in the 'American' style: factual and reflective. If a story like this can now be written about the short career of a Russian pop and dance duo, there can no longer be any excuse for not tackling more substantial artists in the same way.

Patrizio Nissirio*

*Patrizio Nissirio holds a PhD in American Studies (University of Rome, 1995) and is now a professional journalist, having begun his career as a music critic. Currently the Head of ANSAmed, the multilingual agency of ANSA (Agenzia Nazionale Stampa Associata; the Italian press agency) for the Mediterranean, he is also the author of *Dettagli American, Il Paese dietro la bandiera* (Liberali libri, 2002) and *Ouzo Amaro; La tragedia greca Olimpiadi al gol di Samaras* (Fazi, 2012).

INTRODUCTION

A year earlier or a year later, a different tone or some other small detail, and we could have missed... It's like winning 100 million buying a lottery ticket at a newspaper kiosk, except it is even more difficult because the ticket must be produced itself, then that particular ticket must be bought, and no one knows the exact moment.

Boris Rensky, 2012[1]

On a hot summer night in 2012 I found myself by a lucky series of coincidences chatting on Skype to Sven Martin, keyboard player with t.A.T.u. throughout their career, the man who produced the sound on many of their songs, music consultant, writer of *Running Blind,* and a close friend of Lena Katina (with whom he still plays today) and Julia Volkova.

Talking to him about the ups and downs of their ten-year career and about how little of it is known to the majority of people, I suddenly found myself typing, *'I'll write a book about t.A.T.u. some time. People need to know.'* And Sven replied from Los Angeles, *'Good idea!'*

---

[1] *Интервью с Борисом Ренским,* VK Lena Katina's official page vk.com/lenakatinaofficial, July 4, 2012.

The fascinating history of this original and controversial group reads like a novel: what chance of success did they stand - a music project created almost by accident during Russia's post-economic crisis of 1999 by a software entrepreneur and a creative advertising psychologist, having had no previous contact with the world of show business, in a country that had never launched a single pop star into the international arena, funded with a handful of dollars, with no proper record label behind them, and consisting of two teenage girls from a singing school? At the time, any layman would have said, 'none.' But a few years later those two young girls, by that time women, after selling millions of records around the globe and playing live in Europe, Asia and the Americas in front of hundreds of thousands of people from Wembley Arena in London to the Tokyo Dome, were established as 'legends' by the world's biggest television music station (*MTV Legend Award*).

The following pages tell how all this was made possible by the intuition, unscrupulousness and stubbornness of an extraordinary management, the originality of a few songwriters, the talents of a close-knit group of musicians, and above all the unexpected chemical reaction that took place when Lena Katina and Julia Volkova met: their ability to bewitch millions of teenagers with their combined voices and to scandalise a similar number of adults with their appearance, for the entire first decade of the new millennium.

For people who lost interest after their initial worldwide hits, *All The Things She Said* and *Not Gonna Get Us,* t.A.T.u. remain simply 'that scandalous lesbian duo.' But Julia and Lena demonstrated their ability over the years that followed to go far beyond the fictional and commercial image created by their first manager, and achieve excellence in every aspect of their performance, as described succinctly by Roger Holland in his *PopMatters* column:

Emotion offered by Lena and Yulya's quite distinct vocal ranges touches places most pop music couldn't find with a map and GPS.

This book is designed for those who only remember them for their kissing on stage, to help them discover who t.A.T.u. really were, what was behind that provocative, disturbing and commercialised image, and perhaps play some of their CDs again and listen to them impartially.

Friendly contact has been maintained over recent months with many of the characters mentioned; this biography, however, is almost entirely constructed from news reports of the time, press and TV articles, film footage, sound recordings and blogs, as listed in the bibliography, and cannot therefore be considered in any way official or accredited by t.A.T.u.'s artists or management.

THE DAWN OF TATY

God or fate brought us together.
After all, this was what we'd hoped
and prayed for all along.

Lena Katina, 2003[2]

Many people believe that the destiny of every creature born on Earth is already mapped out, in spite of the *'sliding doors'* possibilities that open and close for each one of us every day seeming to suggest the contrary. It is certainly the case for t.A.T.u, who lived more than ten years of their own story in a whirlwind of chance, incidents, setbacks and - fortunately – successes, that can only be explained as being the will of an often generous, and sometimes mocking, fate.

What's more, the way their story begins is also quite unique in the music world: t.A.T.u. do not start out as a group of young artists expressly brought together in their early careers, as was the case with ABBA in Sweden for example, and similarly it is not the brainchild of a music industry professional such as Nigel Martin Smith in the case of Take That in England. What will become the most globally successful Russian group in history is in fact created as a spontaneous chemical reaction when certain individuals come together who are little more than amateurs in the recording world, and certainly have no experience at international level. They are Ivan Nikolaevich Shapovalov (Vanja to his friends), who holds a diploma in child psychology but works successfully as a producer

---

[2] *FLASH Magazine* (Japan), June 2003.

of advertising commercials; Alexander Voitinskyi, a songwriter and colleague of Shapovalov's in the advertising industry; Boris Rensky, an entrepreneur in the IT field for whom Shapovalov has carried out several advertising campaigns and who has become a close friend; Elena Kiper, a TV journalist and amateur singer-songwriter, and Shapovalov's life partner, and finally Sergio Galoyan, a young songwriter and DJ still unknown at the time.

Boris and Vanja agree on a total investment of $60,000 for the entire project: a trifling amount in terms of the western market and which Vanja often displays as a badge of honour to demonstrate his entrepreneurial prowess. But consideration should also be given to the fact that in 1999, the year the project is launched, Russia has just come through a heavy monetary devaluation of the ruble that has seen it drop to a fifth of its previous value against the dollar. Consequently, sixty thousand dollars is now enough to buy a decent apartment in the centre of St. Petersburg or Moscow, and in view of this the figure that Rensky advances to Vanja is anything but trifling.

The initiative comes from Shapovalov with the help of Voitinskyi: the idea is to bring something new to the Russian music scene with the minimum possible investment (the money comes from his friend Boris) and without any great ambition for it to be a lasting thing.

It's the end of 1998. Alex and Vanja audition a lot of young girls, most of whom are from 'Neposedi', a kind of school/music group in Moscow that often does TV performances. By the end of the auditions they have got it down to ten girls and finally just two remain: Elena (Lena) Sergeevna Katina and Yulia (Julia) Olegovna Volkova. Alex is inclined towards Katina whilst Vanja prefers Volkova, and in the end the first of these is chosen.

Lena at this time is still only fourteen. She was born in Moscow on 4 October 1984, the daughter of Sergey Katin, a respected musician, and Inessa Katina. She attends elementary-secondary school no.457 in Moscow and started learning piano at no.30 music school at the age of six. At the age of ten she was a soloist in the children's group Avenue which she left to join Neposedi, where Volkova had already been singing for some time: Lena later remembers being ribbed by Julia for being the 'new girl' in the early days.

When the auditions take place in 1998, for which she sings *It Must Have Been Love* by Roxette, Lena is there almost by accident, as she herself says:

> The Director of Neposedi called us and asked us if we wanted to go to an audition at the Mosfilm studios. I only went because they asked me, I wasn't that interested and didn't think any more about it after I left the studios. (Lena Katina, 2013)[3]

Neither Shapovalov nor Voitinskyi are at the auditions: a Mosfilm technician films the girls on a video camera, asking each one to say something, dance and then sing. Lena is contacted some time later and asked to come back to the studios, where this time Shapovalov asks her to try singing some short songs in different keys. After a few weeks Vanya calls her again and tells her he wants to use one of the recordings for a TV commercial for the soft drink Chernogolovka, offering her $250 as payment.[4]

Eager[5], good-natured and thoughtful, an avid reader of fiction and literature (which will in time increase her predisposition to shortsightedness) and intending to go on to study at university, the young Lena is cheerful and friendly with everyone. If you search the internet for Katina's characteristics and not just her voice, you'll notice how often the adjective 'angelic' comes up, and it's remarkable how often this term is still applied to her today, even

---

[3] Statements by Lena Katina in 2013; no reference to follow as they were spoken in person to the author.

[4] *Караван историй*, December 2011.

[5] Julieta Aguilar, «Lena Katina" *OK! Magazine Mexico*, September 2011.

though she's now twenty-nine, which says a lot about the personality of the young Lena in 1999.

The young Julia, born on 20 October 1985 also in Moscow, daughter of Oleg Volkov, a clerical worker, and Larissa Volkova, is a completely different character. Her first school is elementary school no.882 but she doesn't show much interest in her studies here, then at the age of 11 she moves to 1113, which has special classes in music, on the advice of a neighbour with whom she takes piano and singing lessons, and who sees that she has talent. As she recalls years later, Julia has a difficult time with her tutors, who are intent on stopping her coming to school in make-up and dressed for clubbing. In 1994 she starts at Neposedi, which she leaves in 1998 a few months before the Mosfilm auditions, to enrol on a singing course at Gnessin's State Musical College in Moscow, and not, as Shapovalov claims during t.A.T.u.'s early years, because she is expelled for alleged sexual advances towards some of her fellow students. (This story about harassment at Neposedi was circulated by Shapovalov deliberately, according to a later report by Elena Pindzhoyan[6], a teacher at the school). Feisty, at times rebellious and decidedly impulsive, the young Volkova underneath the armour of these character traits is actually much more sensitive than she appears: you only have to look at her smile, which reveals a barely-concealed insecurity. Julia is no stranger to the entertainment industry when she does the audition in 1998, at which she sings the Russian folk song *Oy, to ne vecher*; in fact she has already had a leading role in several episodes of 'Eralash', a TV series for young people, and is showing a flair for acting that will benefit her in the coming years. Boris Grachevskiy, who directed the series, recalls[7]:

---

[6] Katy Waitz, *"I Prefer Underage Girls "*, *The Sun*, 10 February 2003.

[7] *Closer to the Stars*, MUZ TV, 4 November 2006.

> From the first episode it was a great success. She was wonderful, natural and exact. (Boris Grachevskiy, 2006)

Julia continues to record episodes of 'Eralash' until the end of 2000. Even though she's fifteen by this time she still manages to look thirteen, the age she was when the series started, with her hair in pigtails and a band pulled tight across her breasts to flatten them.

Two months after recording the Chernogolovka commercial, Vanja and Alex invite Lena to another meeting where they ask her to sing some demos. One of these is *Yougoslavia*. It's the spring of 1999, the date of the NATO Allied Forces operation against Slobodan Milosevic's Federal Republic of Yugoslavia, and Voitinskyi wrote the song following the wave of emotion unleashed by the bombing raids. It is Vanya's intention to ask Boris Rensky to finance a TV show against the war, with Russian artists taking part and Lena as the main singer[8]. He aims to stimulate public emotion with this little blonde girl who has the voice of an angel. But when Vanya takes Lena to see Rensky, Rensky is fascinated by her. He rejects the idea of a single show and instead suggests building up a whole music project around the girl. A few days later on 31 May 1999, Lena has her makeup done by Alexander Shevchuk, a promising makeup artist at that time, and poses for a photo shoot. This date is considered to be the official start of 'project Тату.'

At around the same time eighteen-year-old Sergey (Sergio) Galoyan is looking for a suitable music venture to launch the dance songs that he has written; a friend in the music industry recommends him to Vanja and the two meet up in Moscow. Sergio plays some of his pieces for Shapovalov, who is very interested; so much so that he entrusts Sergio with some song lyrics written by

---

[8] Sergey Anisimov, *t.A.T.u.: "Мы и сейчас иногда целуемся", "OK! Magazine Russia*, no.20 (133) 2009.

his girlfriend, Elena Kiper: 'If you like them, write some music to go with them and we'll see what happens[9].'

The story in the lyrics that Vanja gives to Sergio is one that Kiper herself refers to in 2004 during the reality show 't.A.T.u. in Podnebesnaya.[10]' Whilst Elena is ill in hospital and under sedation, she dreams that her colleague on MTV Russia, Tutta Larsen, tries to kiss her. She is noticeably shaken by the experience when she comes round, and addresses her feelings by writing down a few verses on a piece of paper about a girl who, after dreaming about kissing a girl the same age as herself and being in love with her, is no longer able to distinguish between the dream and reality when she wakes up. The verses she writes contain the exclamation *Ya soshla s uma!* ('I've lost my mind!') which will later become the title of Taтy's first single. The perturbing dream experience must have given Elena an idea for redefining the project that her partner was at that time developing, to convert it into a teenage duo with explicit Sapphic references.

It takes Galoyan no more than an hour to adapt one of his tunes to Kiper's lyrics; he prepares a demo but decides to wait at least a week before presenting it to Vanja, to give the impression it has had due consideration. At his second meeting with Shapovalov, Sergio brings the CD and they listen to it together in the car. Vanya likes the demo but tells Galoyan that the project has changed, and that there will probably be two girls singing. 'Even better,' replies Galoyan[11] 'the song will be much sexier with two girls singing it.'

In fact, Vanja later plays down Elena's contribution (conceding that the dream influenced the song[12] and nothing else) claiming that he himself[13] came up with the group's identity. But taking into account that the original lyrics for *Ya Soshla S Uma* were the

---

[9] Quote given by Sergio Galoyan in person to the author.

[10] *t.A.T.u. in Podnebesnaya,* STS TV, Episode 7, 7 February 2004.

[11] Quote given by Sergio Galoyan in person to the author.

[12] *Making of "Ya Soshla S Uma"* Video, Neformat.

[13] *t.A.T.u. in Podnebesnaya,* STS TV, Episode 7, 7 February 2004.

subject of a lawsuit between the two of them in 2003 and 2004, Shapovalov might have changed his version at that time for personal interests. In a February 2003 interview with The Sun[14] in Britain, Vanja claims that he created Тату's identity through simply observing that most adults surf the internet looking for pornography, and underage sex in particular. Many years later, in an interview with the Russian monthly, Karavan[15], Lena gives an entirely different version:

> The film Fucking Amal had just come out, about a love affair between two sixteen-year-old girls and Boris and Ivan began discussing the video, "These two girls fell in love with each other. How can you tell this to your parents? Their former classmates would look at them negatively...They can't even explain this to themselves". Yulia would sometimes get into conversations between Ivan and Boris and in her sweet voice would give her opinion, "Everyone can go screw themselves! And I'd blow up the school to pieces!" "Hm, good idea", responded the new-born producers. (Lena Katina, 2011)

The fact is that whoever the architect was, that idea back in 2000 of launching the image of two teenage schoolgirls singing about their homosexual inclinations and being explicit about them would prove to be positively advantageous to the initial success of the venture.

---

[14] Katy Waitz, *"I Prefer Underage Girls", The Sun, 10 February 2003.*

[15] *Караван историй,* December 2011.

THE BIRTH OF TATY AND YA SOSHLA S UMA

By mid-1999 guidelines for the group project led by Shapovalov have been drawn up: Julia Volkova is called in to sing alongside Lena Katina, they have a subject for the first song (the one outlined by Elena, with the lyrics adapted by Valeriy Polienko) and they also have Sergio's tune. Galoyan has not yet met the girls and asks Vanja if it wouldn't be better to involve them in the arrangement, but Shapovalov thinks differently: 'absolutely not! They're fourteen, they're so young they can hardly speak properly, let alone write music.' (Ivan Shapovalov, 1999)[16]

The early stages of production of the single are described in an interview with Galoyan, published in Resolution[17] magazine in 2005: it's the first real experience for any of them, the technical stuff is very vague, the girls are very young and there's no autotune (software that automatically tunes even dissonant voices to a melody) because it's not widely available yet, but morale is sky high. Everybody's enthusiastic, Julia and Lena are exuberant; it's like we just know we're creating something new and unique.

> They're just fun, they come into the studio and smash everything, tell everybody 'This is my music!' (Sergio Galoyan, 2005)

---

[16]Quote given by Sergio Galoyan in person to the author.

[17] George Shilling, "Sergio *Galoyan," Resolution Magazine,* November/December V4.8 2005.

The two girls are in complete harmony with each other. Lena recalls ten years later[18]:

> It was such careless time. We lived in each other's places – sometimes Yulka stayed with me, sometimes I stayed with her. Sometimes we walked in the city until 4 in the morning and then lied our parents that we were recording in the studio. (Lena Katina, 2009)

Shapovalov is still the undisputed leader of this motley crew that will nevertheless turn out to be a winner. Vanya concerns himself with everything and has yet another eureka moment: if we're staking everything on how young the girls are, we should make sure they sound really adolescent too. So he instructs Julia, who is younger and can reach the high notes more easily, to sing a high-pitched countermelody (probably taking his inspiration from the German female band TicTacToe) over the voice of Lena, which is more mature and so almost always the leading voice. This scheme - Lena the main voice, Julia the secondary voice and chorus/countermelody in a higher key - which also adds some realism to the drama of the lyrics, will prove successful and will often be repeated in later songs, becoming something of a trademark of Тату's early style. Too bad that such an effective plan for the group's success has such a detrimental effect on Julia's vocal chords, which in a little over three years become severely damaged. It is significant that Vanja never saw any need for a vocal coach on the project: he claimed that the girls' way of singing was completely their own without any outside influences and without conforming to any stereotypes, so much so that he would scold Julia all the time for using melisma like she had been

---

[18] Sergey Anisimov, 't.A.T.u.: "Мы и сейчас иногда целуемся", "OK! Magazine Russia, no.20 (133) 2009.

taught by her singing teacher at Gnessin, and would make her sing in a completely different way, as Lena explains:

> You're singing this song like Mariah Carey would sing it, but you have to sing it like Julia Volkova, just like Lena Katina sings like Lena Katina. (Ivan Shapovalov, 1999)[19]

Much has been said about the influence, not always positive, that Shapovalov had over the young Julia. Elena Kiper, in the aforementioned article in The Sun in 2003, does not conceal her jealousy of Volkova: from their very first contact Vanja is strongly attracted to Julia (remember that she was his first choice while Alex preferred Katina), and according to Kiper he has already managed to seduce her in the back seat of his car by the end of the second audition. Julia, of course, is very young at the time but legally able to consent (at the time the age of sexual consent in Russia had just been lowered[20] from 16 to 14, and was put back up to 16 in 2003), Vanja is a good looking thirty-year-old man with great charisma, and above all represents for Julia - who comes from a family of modest means - the road to success. Kiper points out, adding credibility to the circumstances:

> Julia was just a young girl from a poor background looking for fame and fortune and Ivan convinced her that was how she could get it (Elena Kiper, 2003)[21]

Knowing that there was, or was not, an intimate relationship between Julia and Shapovalov (both of them deny the allegations in the article), essentially adds little to the story that we're concerned with here, but the latter undeniably has a profound

---

[19] Quote given by Lena Katina in person to the author.

[20] *Федеральный закон от 25.06.1998 N 92-ФЗ*. Consultant.ru. 25 June 1998.

[21] Katy Weitz, *"I Prefer Underage Girls"*, The Sun, February 10, 2003.

influence on the two young girls. Lena admits as much many years later[22]:

> I was only thirteen when I met Ivan, and he soon became an authority figure for me that he could have put any idea in my head. But, thank God Ivan was a different person back then, much more modest. He had not imagined himself as God. (Lena Katina, 2012)

Vanja - let's not forget - is a psychologist and trained to engage the trust of his patients: Kiper herself admits to having fallen at one time into the same trap that the much more defenseless Julia and Lena fall into later. Galoyan, with whom the girls record all their debut tracks, goes as far as to describe Shapovalov's control over Julia and Lena as almost hypnotic[23]. The charismatic Vanja acts like a real puppet master with the two girls: right up to the moment the contract is signed, their parents (Shapovalov himself admits it[24]) are unaware that the girls will have to pretend to be lesbians and pledge not to make public statements about their sexual orientation. This clause will be crucial in supporting the fabricated story of a supposed homosexual relationship between the two.

Before *Ya Soshla S Uma* is released - which will officially take place in December 2000 - Vanja wants to fine tune every detail, starting of course with the name of the group. The choice of name shows that the expectations of success that Shapovalov and his companions had for the group, as confirmed years later by the financier Boris Rensky[25], do not extend beyond the borders of Russia. The name ТАТУ [*author's note*: pronunced ta'tu] is

---

[22] Eugene Levkovich, *"Площадь Ленина," Rolling Stone Magazine Russia,* June 2012.

[23] Anna Veligzhanina *"Композитор Сергей Галоян:" ТАТУ "СТАЛИ лесбиянками под гипнозом," Komsomolskaya Pravda,* 20 March 2003.

[24] Katy Weitz,"I Prefer Underage Girls",The Sun, February 10, 2003.

[25] *Интервью с Борисом Ренским,* VK, Lena Katina's official page vk.com/lenakatinaofficial, July 4, 2012.

recognisable only to Russian mother-tongue speakers and is a compound of the feminine pronoun TA ('this' in the nominative) and TY ('that' in the accusative) which means 'this (girl) [does something] to that (girl)' and later widely interpreted as 'this girl loves that girl.' The choice will prove to be inspired and effective, but will cause problems a year later when the huge success of the song carries the name of the group over the border and it's realised too late that there is already an Australian band called Tatu (made up of three girls, oddly enough, who have come up through the talent show 'Popstars'[26]), and whose most famous single - so to speak - is *Imperfect Girl*. For this reason the new and definitive format with full stops is adopted: *t.A.T.u.* with the two central letters in uppercase and the one at each end in lowercase to make the name even more identifiable as a brand, along the same lines as ABBA in the 70s, with the first B reversed. In some countries the trade mark t.A.T.u. is actually registered by T.A. Music under the 'education and entertainment services' sector[27].

In the meantime Julia and Lena, who are also taking dance lessons in preparation for future live performances, continue to record studio demos of the other songs that will make up their first album. Vanja, Elena and Alex together with Sergio have selected the entire repertoire that he had ready (enough for three albums) by taking the tune from one song, the sound from another, and so on, building up the foundations for the creation of *Nas Ne Dogonyat, 30 Minut, Ya Tvoya Ne Pervaya* and *Mal'chik-Gey*.

In early 2000 the final version of *Ya Soshla S Uma* is now ready and Shapovalov starts going round all the radio stations in Moscow plugging the song, but as Boris says ten years later[28], he gets the same answer from all of them: 'the song is boring, unprofessional and not suitable for radio broadcasting.' On top of that Boris and

---

[26] *"Popstars II: Over to Oz" The New Zealand Herald,* 29 April 2000.

[27] U.S. trademark serial number 76405350, EU Community Trade Mark number 002 921 195.

[28] Official Tatu.ru blog, post by *Insider,* 20 November 2010.

Vanja are two complete strangers in the music world and as someone points out, the problem is not with the song, but with the lack of credibility of those promoting it. Boris even offers a 25% share in the project in exchange for playing the song, to a childhood friend now working for a major broadcaster in Moscow, but he turns the offer down, believing there to be no future for it.

But they can't be defeated at this stage: Vanja has already spent half of the $60,000 that Boris made available to him and has only $30,000 left to make a video; a totally inadequate amount even in Russia at that time. The last chance according to Shapovalov's plan, in fact, is to release a video that will drive home the story that they've constructed around the group: a story that will shock adolescents (especially girls) and scandalise adults. In short, it has to be explosive enough to blast Vanja's manufactured image of a sensational, erotic 'teenage lesbian duo' far and wide.

And who if not Shapovalov himself, with his experience in communications and his natural magnetism for teenagers (by his own admission), can concieve and produce such a video? Funds, as we know, are in short supply: Hodinskoe Field (Khodynka Field) in the suburbs northwest of Moscow is chosen as the location: a featureless area once used as an airfield. In early September a crew of a few dozen people (the young background actors are Galoyan's classmates) build a mock-up of a brick wall out of wire fencing, no more than eight metres long and four metres high, covered in graffiti, topped with barbed wire and aged with spray paint, and they prepare lots and lots of water[29].

When Lena and Julia arrive on the set they already have the look that they've rehearsed with Shapovalov. Lena has been on a strict diet[30] and has lost about ten kilos compared to what she weighed the year before, (she has to look two or three years younger than

---

[29] *Making of "Ya Soshla S Uma"*, Video, Neformat.

[30] *"В любовь с Волковой я не играла. Все было по-настоящему"*, *Moskovsky Komsomolets* no. 25760, 1 October 2011.

her actual age of sixteen). Her red hair has been bleached for the occasion (in t.A.T.u.'s early years she tends to keep the platinum shade and goes back to her natural colour later) and she still has the natural curls that she appeared on TV with when she was at Neposedi. In Vanya's plan Lena is the femminine one of the couple so she has to look helpless and angelic. Julia, on the other hand, has to iconify the more androgynous one and is forced to give up her blond hair and become almost raven black with a cropped style that brings out her blue eyes and striking looks, and makes her look a lot younger than her fifteen years, on Shapovalov's orders. A few years later Julia confesses that at the time she used to sit for long periods in front of the mirror, seeing a child's reflection instead of her own.[31].

Vanja makes Julia and Lena wear what has to appear to be a Catholic secondary school uniform: long-sleeved white blouse, short pleated tartan skirt, tie, and a different style of flat shoes for each girl: shiny ballerinas with buckles for Lena who is the taller of the two, whilst Julia gains a few centimetres with thick rubber-soled boots. The trick of wearing different shoes will also be used later in the first few photo shoots. A few years later the Russian designer Andrey Drykin reveals[32] that he created the schoolgirl look on the instructions of Elena Kiper.

But it's the water that provides the final touch to the video: Vanja places the girls in front of the wall, like prisoners outside a perimeter enclosure in the pouring rain. The end result is impressive: whilst Lena and Julia are singing at the tops of their voices, chilled to the bone and shivering from the cold water - as they recall in the behind-the-scenes video - they really *do* turn into two frightened little twelve-year-olds! This is the true magic of Shapovalov: the observer doesn't see a music video shot in the

---

[31] *t.A.T.u. Life*, Russia.ru TV, Episode 4.

[32] Elena Karpenko *"Парень из провинциальной Рязани" делал лицо "Пэлтроу и Линде Евангелисте"*, *Vechernyaya Moskva*, June 16, 2005.

studios, but two little girls numb with cold, crying out against the exponents of a bigoted and moralistic society trying to prevent the natural and innocent love they have for one another. And notwithstanding a couple of cheeky shots from below that reveal the girls' underwear, Shapovalov manages not to overdo the eroticism which would be counter-productive; an incredible feat for a character like him. It's true, Julia and Lena do kiss, but there are no explicit sexual references: it's the image of a first innocent kiss between two teenagers, and it's irrelevant that those teenagers are of the same sex.

As Shapovalov himself says[33] 'This video is the birth of Тату': the project, the music, the lyrics, the voices... more than an entire year's work would have been completely useless without this video: Тату were really born on 4 September 2000 with the first take of the *Ya Soshla S Uma* video.

In spite of the excellent work, however, the music stations are apparently not interested in broadcasting the video, and it is systematically turned down. Once again Vanja and Boris suffer for their complete inexperience in show business, but finally one day when Shapovalov has turned up at the MTV Russia offices for the umpteenth time, the head of local programming admits that the clip has a certain appeal and although he doesn't think it will have much success he decides to show it a few times for a limited period starting in November.

Just seven days after its release the video has an enormous public following; it reaches number one in the MTV Russia charts and is played more than 35 times a week. Musician Jean-Sebastien Decarie later writes this review[34]:

> What is Oh So Great about Tatu, is that their videos totally represent their lyrics. No teenagers trashing cars and whatnot

---

[33] *Making of "Ya Soshla S Uma"* Video, Neformat.

[34] Mycdreviews.com, 28 November 2002.

singing a song that doesn't have anything to do with trashing cars [*author's note: the reference is to the Sk8er Boi video by Avril Lavigne*]. I already loved their music, and the conviction to stick to what the lyrics means in their videos appealed to me instantly!

On November 26 at Club 5 Element in Moscow, Тату perform (lip-synching) for the first time, and also kiss in public for the first time. On stage, the girls still seem uncertain how to behave: Julia, with her unusual dark brown hair (she had to go back to blonde to record the final episode of 'Eralash' after filming the video for *Ya Soshla S Uma,* and hasn't got it back to the full black yet) is a bit more mobile than the timid Lena, who is wearing a watch on her left wrist which Vanja had expressly forbidden. After the manager remonstrates with her, she doesn't wear it on stage any more.

As Shapovalov expected, broadcasting the song and video on TV and the internet has an immediate effect: the press and the Russian media are suddenly interested in these two unknown young girls professing lesbian love and kissing in public. Vanja instructs his two creatures pointedly and minutely on how to behave from now on: very few autographs and no particular dedications - just the signature; avoid using terms of endearment – 'dear' etc; always write 'Тату' after the signature. At press conferences their answers must be brief and they must not talk about other music; Julia must not talk about literature because she hates it, and Lena must not mention her favorite books. They should always avoid questions relating to their sexual preferences, sex in general and their life together. Lena and Julia are contractually obliged to give interviews as part of their work, so they have to respond appropriately for the first 20 minutes of the interview, after which they may say they've had enough and bring it to an end if they wish.

But for a few months Shapovalov strategically avoids letting Lena and Julia give any interviews at all except for press conferences.

His aim is to release as little information as possible and to make the public and the media clamour for more details about the two girls who appeared from nowhere and are causing such a stir.

TOWARDS 200 PO VSTRECHNOY

On 19 December 2000, two months after their debut, the group's first official press conference is held at secondary school 1113 in Moscow, and their first 'mini album' is released (it's actually a single/EP) which includes the single *Ya Soshla S Uma*, two videos and 4 remix versions. This first CD by Тату, released on the independent Neformat label set up by Boris and Vanya, sells 50,000 copies in next to no time.

Lena and Julia arrive radiant aboard a van at the entrance to the same school that Julia goes to, and are greeted by a small crowd of kids and reporters. Shapovalov is with them of course, and remains seated next to the girls throughout the press conference, behind a desk on the little stage. Naturally, Julia and Lena, who in jeans and sweaters and with the same hairstyles as they had in the *Ya Soshla S Uma* video still appear younger than they actually are, maintain physical contact with each other the whole time: Julia is photographed sitting on Lena's knee, hugging her and stroking her hair. They even indulge in a kiss that has already become Тату's 'trademark'.

Vanja's direction of the event is without doubt a success: first, the choice of a secondary school as the venue for the press conference, emphasising the youth of the girls and their distance from show-business, and allowing adolescents - the main consumers of this type of music - to identify with them. And the naturalness of Julia and Lena, who at their first real public appearance manage to adopt the Тату characteristics exactly as Shapovalov envisaged them: sweet and natural, provocative and inviting, but naive and often shy at the same time. The idea that their loving relationship might be a pretence doesn't even enter the minds of the kids who are watching them, intrigued, fascinated and a little bit unsettled. In fact, the instinctive question we ask ourselves today is whether it's possible Vanja was such a clever strategist and psychologist as to get Julia and Lena to play their parts with such spontaneity and credibility. Of course Julia had already demonstrated her talent for acting, as we have seen, and of the two of them it's Julia - and always will be Julia - who makes more physical contact and is more forthcoming in her demonstrations of affection for Lena. But is it really all pretence? Or after more than a year of living in close daily contact, sharing joyful enthusiasm for what they were creating, harmonising with each other's voices, laughing together, and probably (knowing Vanya's determination) occasionally crying together, professing - at least in their songs - mutual love whilst gazing into each other's eyes and holding hands, and of course for the boisterous and instinctive Julia to be able to lean on the placidity of Lena, and for Lena to be able to count on the determined and unpredictable character of Julia to defend her, surely an affection must have blossomed that went deeper than just a sincere and platonic friendship? Psychologist Irina Sakovnia states in the 2006 MUZ-TV television investigation 'Closer to the Stars':

> The girls turned out to be really talented, because they didn't just limit themselves to acting out what they were asked, they actually lived it. Obviously, that required an enormous emotional undertaking. (Irina Sakovnia, 2006)

Julia and Lena were so convincing that Lena's own mother found herself more than once in those days asking her daughter if fiction had become reality[35].

---

[35] Eugene Levkovich, *"Площадь Ленина"*, *Rolling Stone Magazine Russia*, June 2012.

In 2003, remembering this initial period in the documentary 'Anatomy of t.A.T.u.'[36], Lena admits, whilst reiterating that she was still heterosexual:

> I still don't understand how I managed to overcome my profound reluctance. I told myself that we had to kiss just for the publicity, nothing more. My mother explained to me that at that age, 14 or 15 when a girl has a best friend, it's often hard to identify what she feels for her, whether it's friendship or love: there's a little-understood feeling between the two and they're divided by such a fine line. (Lena Katina, 2003)

In the years ahead Lena and Julia will of course become increasingly dependent on each other and at the end of their journey together we will witness a profound crisis of separation on Lena's part. Because of this, and in spite of the declarations made in the 2003 documentary 'Anatomy of t.A.T.u.' mentioned above, in which the girls finally admit that their alleged homosexual relationship was just dramatised fiction (Lena more forcefully than Julia), many fans will continue to consider their demonstrations of mutual affection sincere.

> We often kissed even when we were not in public [...] but we never had sex with each other, not once. (Lena Katina, 2012)[37]

While psychologists and commentators, of course, take it upon themselves to label the Sapphic message of *Ya Soshla S Uma* as sensitive and potentially harmful to minors[38], the Russian press shows an interest in the unexpected Тату phenomenon[39] and all in

---

[36] Vitaly Mansky (director) *Анатомия ТАТУ*, STS TV, 12 December 2003.

[37] Eugene Levkovich, *"Площадь Ленина"*, *Rolling Stone Magazine Russia*, June 2012.

[38] Alexander Bratersky, *"Tatu's Teen Queens"*, *The Moscow Times*, 7 June 2001.

[39] *"Пятнашки"*, *Evening Moscow*, 22 December 2000.

all is not too scandalised but simply questions whether the two young girls will be able to produce anything else and if they will ever perform live on stage; in short, if it's just a short-lived success or if indeed something new and lasting has been born.

Shapovalov already knows the answer to these questions. Their first experiment is going extremely well and Tату's market value is now such that they can have no hesitation in approaching an established record label to produce their first album, and in a short time an agreement is signed with the Russian division of Universal who envisage the release of three albums by the end of 2002. Despite their excellent prospects however, the Tату 'clan' is already starting to fall apart: Alex Voitinskyi has stepped down and Vanya has decided to replace him by promoting his partner Elena from just co-writer of lyrics to the role of co-producer. Universal also expects a more finished product than the first version of *Ya Soshla S Uma* for the debut album, and for this reason has hired expert Trevor Horn (who played in successful bands like the Buggles and Yes as well as producing the Pet Shop Boys and other famous British bands) who wants, among other things, to rerecord the original song before putting it on the album scheduled for release next spring. The new version will be recorded in Manchester.

In the meantime Julia and Lena, as well as making studio recordings of the new songs, perform in public in February in Odessa (their first concert outside Russia), Yekaterinburg, Rostov and St. Petersburg, and participate in the Babiy Concert at Moscow's Kremlin Hall on 17th March. The whole concert is filmed by MTV Russia, to be broadcast two days later: this is Tату's very first live television appearance where *Ya Soshla S Uma* is performed (they are actually lip-synching and their own voices are superimposed over parts of it), and the first time in public (and on TV) that *Nas Ne Dogonyat* is performed. Tату are let loose: they run up and down the enormous stage in the same schoolgirl uniforms as they wore for the *Ya Soshla S Uma* video, hugging and kissing several times, and towards the end of the performance Lena gets to tear Julia's blouse off. This was obviously staged since Julia is wearing a demure flesh-coloured bra underneath, but it sends the crowd of kids in the audience into a frenzy as well as those watching at home on TV. In one fell swoop Тату answer two of the questions that the press had posed: yes, we can play live and wow the audience, and no, *Ya Soshla S Uma* will not be an isolated success. The new song is indeed powerful, intriguing, and a natural sequel to *Ya Soshla S Uma*, including the plotline - about two young girls in love and running away together to escape from people trying to break them up.

> Shapovalov had teenagers in mind as the target audience for our music. Our image had been calculated for this purpose, to epitomise two teenagers prepared to stand up to everything and everyone. (Lena Katina, 2013)

Filming for the *Nas Ne Dogonyat* video starts on 20 February – Julia's 16th birthday - when the area around Moscow is covered in a thick blanket of snow (the set is near an old airport in the small town of Dmitrov, 65km north of the capital) and it snows on almost every day of the shoot, which lends the images some authenticity. Directed once again by Shapovalov, this time the girls are portrayed running away from an airport after being arrested and charged by the police for an unspecified crime. This video is much more complex and eventful than the one for *Ya Soshla S Uma* (the productions costs are $90,000 as opposed to $30,000 for the first video[40]), and much of it is shot on an enormous truck driving along an endless straight road running alongside a forest, reminiscent of the final scene of Andron Konchalovsky's film, *Runaway Train.* Vanja, who carves out a cameo role for himself playing the

---

[40] *"МК "посчитал, сколько стоят звезды",* Moskovsky Komsomolets, 10 February 2006

workman run over by Julia who takes the wheel, again has no hesitation in exposing his two creatures to the freezing cold and snow (the temperature was -20° as Lena recalls in an interview[41]), only excusing them from the most dangerous scenes where they balance on the roof of the moving truck (in the behind-the-scenes video[42] there is also a short interview with Lena's stuntwoman). In the final version the moving images are alternated with very brief shots of Lena and Julia in real life, and members of their families. In this way the skilful Shapovalov convinces his young audience in an almost subliminal way to increasingly identify the stars of the video with the girls who play them: in the subconscious minds of teenagers, those girls on the runaway truck are Lena and Julia: they're singing about a real event - they're talking about the real love they have for one another.

The month of May 2001 represents a milestone in Тату's history: on the 16th the contract with Universal is officially announced at the Radisson-Slavyanskaya Hotel in Moscow; Universal becomes Тату's record label and opens the door to international distribution in the future; just 5 days later their first album, *200 po Vstrechnoy*, and the *Nas Ne Dogonyat* video are released simultaneously.

The highly anticipated debut album, on the cover of which Julia and Lena appear in four mugshots similar to those in the opening shots of the *Nas Ne Dogonyat* video, contains *Nas Ne Dogonyat,* the new version of *Ya Soshla S Uma* produced by Trevor Horn, and the songs *Zachem Ya, Doschitay Do Sta, Ya Tvoy Vrag, Ya Tvoya Ne Pervaya, Robot, Mal'chik-Gey* and importantly, *30 Minut* (also known as *Polchasa),* destined to become Тату's third single according to Shapovalov's plan.

Album sales in Russia exceed 500,000 official copies in the first month, and overall sales are way above one million; an impressive figure considering that distribution is handled almost entirely

---

[41] *Total Request Live,* MTV Italy, 15 November 2002.
[42] *Making of "Nas Ne Dogonyat"* Video, Neformat.

inside Russia. Illegal copies which are very common at the time especially among young people, have to be taken into account when comparing these figures with record sales of artists in previous years: this is still pre-iTunes (which launches in 2003) and downloadable music is still scarcely known (the first iPod comes out in 2001). So the cheapest way to enjoy music is with illegal copies, easily made with a tape recorder and also often sold by street vendors. Statistics at the time estimate that there are four illegal copies for each original CD sold.

Immediately following the release of the album Тату begin their *200 po Vstrechnoy Tour* in Russia. The shows, which go on for almost two years outside the homeland too, stick quite closely to Shapovalov's meticulously arranged original format:

1. *Ya Soshla S Uma* playing in the background without the girls on stage; they come on dressed as for the *Ya Soshla S Uma video*.

2. Original version of *Ya Soshla S Uma* .

3. *Zachem Ya* with Lena sitting on the floor and Julia beside her. At the end of the song, Lena and Julia interacting with the audience begin to take off their ties, skirts and blouses. Down to their vests and pants they resume singing:

4. *Ya Tvoya Ne Pervaya.*

5. *30 Minut* Because the song is slow and there is no scene to portray, Lena and Julia have to emphasise their facial expressions, make them more dramatic and engage in physical contact with each other.

6. *Nas Ne Dogonyat.*

7. *Doschitai Do Sta*

8. *Robot.*

A break and a game involving the audience (usually a kissing game) conducted by Julia.

9. *Ya Tvoi Vrag* For this song Vanja recommends that the girl who is not singing should lower her head, and the girl who is singing should bend forward at least 90 degrees to achieve the desired configuration.

10. *Mal'chik-Gey* The movements for this song are similar to the previous one, so the girls will have to introduce some minor variations.

11. *30 Minut* Remix.

12. *Nas Ne Dogonyat.*

During the tour Lena and Julia are accompanied by a small troupe of young dancers alongside whom they also dance themselves, demonstrating their own skills which they learned in dance and artistic gymnastic classes at school. However, because they have to dance, this means it will be almost mandatory to lip-sync for most of the show, but Тату's followers don't seem too concerned about it.

30 MINUT (POLCHASA)

The first official signs of success start to arrive in June: Тату win the '100 Pound Hit' prize for the song *Nas Ne Dogonyat* from the Hit FM radio station (the awards ceremony takes place at the Kremlin Hall where they perform *Ya Soshla S Uma*) and then they win the award for 'Best Hit Song' at the Musical Podium.

The video for *30 Minut* is also recorded in June. As usual Shapovalov's plan is to make the video a mini movie with a precise plot: Julia is a student who, after seeing the girl she loves betray her with a boy, decides to kill them both by hiding a homemade bomb in her lover's backpack. With reference to the lyrics, Julia adjusts the timer of the bomb to 30 minutes ('polchasa' полчаса, translates as 'half an hour') to give Lena one last desperate chance to leave the boy and go back to her. The time passes in vain though, and the bomb destroys the carousel where the couple are having fun, putting an end to the lives of all the characters.

Unfortunately, the behind-the-scenes video[43] shows only the outdoors shots of the carousel and not those inside the school where the Julia's character prepares the bomb. Backstage, Julia often looks bored (she only appears in a couple of reverse shots in the outdoor scenes), while Lena seems to be having fun shooting a love scene with (finally) a boy. The script also includes partial nudity for Lena, who has to appear topless in the boy's arms. It is not known whether the decision to use a stunt double for the nude scene - which is evident from the behind-the-scenes video - was

---

[43] *Making of "30 Minut"* Video, Neformat.

suggested to Vanya because Lena hadn't reached the age of majority at the time of filming.

The end result is once again captivating and engaging: despite the simplicity of the plot, the video adds further drama to the song which already has a moving tune and lyrics, thanks to careful editing, Julia's expressiveness, and the realism of the final scene which is performed without any special effects, actually blowing the carousel up with explosives.

A special note is included at the start of the video: when the English version comes out in 2003 (which doesn't require any re-editing since the girls don't sing in the original video), you don't hear the phrase that Julia murmurs in the background (some people say by mistake) *'mama, papa, forgive me'* which on the English edition of the audio CD is included at the end of the previous track and not at the beginning of *30 Minutes*. This is to dispel one of the Hamletic doubts that fans have been pondering for years - whether the phrase belongs to *30 Minutes* or not.

The track *30 Minut* is officially released as a single in September 2001, and achieves success: it is on the most frequent playlists (more than 30 plays a week) of the major Russian FM stations (Russian Radio, Dinamit, Evropa+, Love Radio, RDV, HIT FM and Tango), while the video remains stable at the top of the charts on MTV Russia and MUZ TV throughout the autumn and winter.

In the meantime Lena and Julia have been working since August on the English language versions of their songs in between stages of their tour, in preparation for the forthcoming international launch. Shapovalov engages a professor from the English language department at Moscow State University to improve the girls' pronunciation (especially Julia's, who knows only a few words of English).

On 3rd September comes the news that Taтy have been chosen by MTV Russia viewers to represent their country in the category 'videos voted for by the public', in the prestigious MTV Video

41

Music Awards scheduled to take place a short time later at the Metropolitan Opera in New York. Julia and Lena rush onto the stage like two rowdy and rebellious troublemakers, Julia grabs the prize, thanks viewers in her own country for the award (in Russian), says goodbye (also in Russian) and runs off with Lena, laughing.

In their first proper international appearance Тату have already revealed what is likely to be the major handicap to their potential real success on a global scale, a handicap that Shapovalov will never succeed in curing (indeed, he possibly makes it worse): their lack of diplomacy. You can't go to a foreign country for a TV ceremony that is being broadcast in practically every country in the world, and accept a prize, even though it was voted for at national level only, without thanking the audience there in front of you and the international audience watching at home in the local language, which is after all English - not some little-known language such as Swahili! It's true that Julia doesn't speak a word of anything but Russian, but Lena does, and both of them know that they're going to be catapulted onto the world stage in the months to come, so what reason is there for such provincialism? Vanya is normally so pernickety about coaching his two creatures for every public appearance they make; he could at least have told them to say 'Hello New York.' This is just the first in a never-ending series of gaffes (amongst other things) that seriously undermine Тату's international career - t.A.T.u.: the success they have outside Russia will be significant but will fall way below their potential, and what they do have owes everything to the captivating power of their music, the innovative and provocative message of the lyrics, their style - irresistible to teenagers (especially female) and of course the sincere naivety that prevents them appearing distant and unapproachable like western pop stars. That's what I would personally call 'tatuism': a winning set of component characteristics but badly compromised by poor reliability, respect for the system, diplomacy and punctuality. A kind of inveterate snobbery against show-business that will forever limit the success of our two darlings (and curtail their solo careers after ten years). But that's not all: tatuismo will prove contagious and will permeate through other, completely separate ventures that revolve around Тату in the years to follow, such as the film *You and I* (which suffers an endless series of setbacks and delays in its distribution, so much so that it never really appears on screens outside Russia).

OUTSIDE THE BORDERS

In autumn 2001 Тату start to move away from Russia (and the former Soviet states) towards the rest of Europe: in October, *Ya Soshla S Uma* is officially released in Slovakia, Czech Republic, Poland and Bulgaria and is an instant success. The following month it's *Nas Ne Dogonyat*, the video for which becomes the no.1 hit on the Bulgarian music station MM Channel in a single day. The album *200 po Vstrechnoy* is released at roughly the same time and immediately becomes the best selling CD in the Czech Republic, Slovakia and Bulgaria.

It is now time for Тату to step through the former Iron Curtain and conquer the West: at the end of 2001 Shapovalov finalises details for the production and launch of *200 Km/h in the Wrong Lane* in English with the general manager of Interscope, a subsidiary of Universal. Russia's association of phonographers officially records *200 po Vstrechnoy* as the best-selling album in Russia of 2001, and in January 2002 Lena and Julia begin their travels to record English versions of their songs in preparation for the launch in Europe and the United States, starting in Germany where they have already performed several times during December, singing in Russian; their record label here is Universal Germany.

On 15th January Lena and Julia are in London where they meet Trevor Horn, and later in Manchester to work with the FAF/Capcom team.

On 15th February Universal releases two new editions of *200 po Vstrechnoy* in Russia to keep public interest alive a year after the original release; still under the name Тату, but with a new cover with a white background. The standard edition contains two remixes and a new track, *Klouny*, as well as the original tracks, while the limited edition also contains the *30 minut* video and new photos of the girls. 60,000 copies of the new edition are sold in the first week alone.

On 18th February Lena and Julia appear alongside Bill Roedy, the manager of MTV (and Jolin Tsai, the Taiwanese Mandopop singer) on the cover of the European edition of prestigious weekly, Business Week[44]. The group's name on the photo caption is Tatu.

The recording sessions for *200 Km/h in the Wrong Lane* start in earnest from 15th March in London at the SARM West Studios with Trevor Horn, and from the 24th in Los Angeles where *Not Gonna Get Us, Clowns, Malchik Gay, I Am Not Your First* and *Show Me Love* are recorded at the Interscope studios. In the breaks between recording sessions in California (during which they also have extra English lessons) Lena and Julia have fun just like any other two young girls, roller blading along Venice Beach. It's a great time for Тату who have some of the best technicians in the world to record their debut international album. Interscope meanwhile also tries to put together a real band for Julia and Lena: Sven Martin (keyboards) and Troy Maccubbin (guitar) are already playing together in Life, Death & Giants when the recording company contacts them to ask them to join t.A.T.u. Roman Ratej (drums) joins them soon after.

> A friend of mine at Interscope phoned me and said 'they're putting together a band for some big deal from Russia - two girls a bit out of the ordinary...we need a keyboard player.' I wasn't that bothered and told him I had my own band and wasn't interested. The next day he called me again and said, 'seriously Sven, won't you just think about this proposal'. So I asked him to send me a CD and just two hours later I was listening to *All The*

---

[44] Business Week European Edition, 18 February 2002.

Things She Said and *Not Gonna Get Us.* I thought, 'Damn, they're really good.' (Sven Martin, 2012)[45]

In April t.A.T.u. receive the 'Bed of the Year Award' in Moscow, in the category Sex Dissidents: the prize consists of a few condoms and Julia asks ironically in front of the microphone: 'What would we need these for?' Lena replies: 'Probably for our collection.'

On 12th April, a few months after Tatу's international launch, Elena Kiper - PR, co-producer and co-writer - suddenly leaves the group. She is replaced by Beata Andreeva, a former VJ with MTV Russia. The official reasons for the break-up are not released, but a year later Kiper brings local civil proceedings to get her rights recognised on Tatу's songs.

On 15th April recording of the new single *Prostye Dvizheniya* is completed and the video for it is shown at the Marika Club in Moscow on 30th May. The video is highly provocative; a presumably naked Julia (the picture stays in close-up because Julia is still a minor, but the outtakes show that she was in fact topless) films herself with a video camera in the bathroom, thinking about Lena who is far away (images of the two are alternated and show Lena sitting pensively in a tearoom, looking at a baby carriage outside on the pavement). The lyrics leave much to the imagination, talking about 'simple movements' without any kind of sexual allusions, but Shapovalov makes it quite explicit in the video, with Julia making movements as if masturbating in front of the camera. It is the first Tatу video in which Shapovalov shows images (albeit soft images) of a sexual act that is not just simple a exchange of affections. Nevertheless, the video for *Prostye Dvizheniya* turns out to be perhaps the least interesting Tatу video and the song itself is one of the least memorable. In fact no English version is never released (the song *A Simple Motion* only appears

---

[45] Statements by Sven Martin 2012 and 2013; no reference to follow as they were spoken in person to the author

on the 2012 commemorative edition of *200 Km/h in the Wrong Lane).* To deflect any kind of accusation against him, Vanja declares publicly[46] that the scene with Julia topless was shot by Julia herself alone in the bathroom with a small camcorder.

On 16th April Тату are in Tel Aviv for their eagerly awaited concert in Israel. The concert - which takes place on national independence day - has the significant title Love Against War and is a sellout. Security measures for protecting the girls are impressive: there are more than 100 men, a helicopter and a number of police patrols.

Two days later on returning to Moscow Lena is suddenly taken ill, presumably because of the constant changes of climate, and the planned concert in the Russian city of Chukotka is cancelled.

After Lena's recovery Тату resume their tour with five concerts in Germany, and on 15th May they are presented with their first European platinum disc[47] for selling a million copies of *200 po Vstrechnoy* at an award ceremony in Moscow (never before achieved by any Eastern European artist). Julia and Lena then leave for Bulgaria where a concert is scheduled for the 22nd in Plovdiv, but it never takes place. Just two hours before the concert the mayor of the city revokes his authorisation of the event, citing the organisation's non-compliance with safety requirements, whereas in fact, as local newspapers[48] reveal the next day, orders are received from the top to prevent the 'scandalous' and uninhibited Russian duo from performing in front of an audience composed mainly of young people. It is worth mentioning as a footnote that Pope John Paul II was due to commence his pastoral visit of Bulgaria the following day, with one of the most important stages actually taking place in Plovdiv.

---

[46] *"Оргазмические бэйбы."*, *Moskovsky Komsomolets*, 29 May 2002.

[47] *"Российский поп-дуэт"* ТАТУ *"удостоен IFPI Platinum Europe Award"*, *Universal Music news*, May 8, 2002.

[48] *"Оргазмические бэйбы"*, *Moskovsky Komsomolets*, 29 May 2002.

This is not the only setback on the tour: the turnout is below expectations at more than one venue, such as Baku, Azerbaijan in January 2002, where large sections of seating in the hall remain empty despite the enormous popularity that Тату have been experiencing there. Amongst the causes outside those attributable to the organisation of the event, no doubt, is the fact that it is aimed with millimetre precision at a target audience composed almost entirely of teenagers: great for CD sales, but teenagers have limited freedom of movement to attend live events, especially in certain Eastern European countries such as Azerbaijan, where the prevailing religion is Islam. For many parents, sending their thirteen-year-old daughters to watch a show by two pseudo-adolescent girls singing about their homosexual love, who rebel against everything and everybody in their videos, stage a reckless escape that involves running over people with a truck, and finally blow themselves up over a mere disappointment in love, clearly doesn't sit at all well.

Plovdiv and Baku prove to be just the early symptoms. Тату soon become aware, in fact, that outside of mother Russia the diabolical pact to which they owe their success, signed on their behalf by Shapovalov when he invented the 'teenage lesbian duo' as they are often labelled in the West, will deeply and irrevocably undermine their future as artists (not forgetting the concept of 'tatuism' too), and even their sudden, desperate and tardy attempt to backpedal a year later is in vain.

But in 2002, 'battleship Тату', fortified by its initial successes, is sailing at full speed toward its destiny, like the glorious *Aurora* in St. Petersburg. An article[49] published in Express Gazeta on 13th May and accompanied by explicit photos, tells what happened at the Park Avenue Disco Nightclub in Moscow, where Тату were to perform. Because they are late arriving on stage (as usual) and because the hall is overcrowded, tempers get a bit overheated so

---

[49] Anton Saveliev *"Вакханалия на концерте 'ТАТУ'"*, Express Gazeta 13 May 2002.

Lena and Julia have the bright idea of inviting people to undress. Many youngsters take the invitation seriously, climb up on stage and are soon completely naked and exchanging displays of affection with each other, transforming the show in no time into what one newspaper decribes as 'a veritable orgy.' Calm is restored with difficulty after security staff intervene, and Тату announce that the show is suspended and that they intend to cancel all future performances at nightclub venues. The magazine Mir Novostei even speculates that there may be claims for damages from parents of underage children who witnessed the 'morally damaging' show.

In June Lena and Julia go back to the US to take part in MTV USA's daily TRL Show in New York and then to Los Angeles to complete some recordings.

Тату return to Moscow on the first of July where a re-shooting of the video for the English version of *Ya Soshla S Uma,* entitled *All The Things She Said,* is scheduled. It is reported that in an attempt to make the new sections indistinguishable from the original, at least part of the fake wall in the background was reconstructed using similar artwork, but one of the original metal nets was still available, so was used again[50]. It's not a simple task: the new sections of video have to be practically indistinguishable from the rest of the shots taken two years before under different conditions. Shapovalov does everything he can to make Lena and Julia look thirteen again, but the result, whilst commendable, doesn't meet to his expectations and he decides not to use the new material (of which some sequences are available on the internet). A frame-by-frame analysis of the new video for *All The Things She Said* shows no new images compared to the 2000 version, just different editing and the use of some outtakes from the previous video from which Shapovalov has taken steps to remove the vocals or to use part of the original sequence where lip movements are compatible with

---

[50] *Accès Privé* M6 TV, November 24, 2012 .

the new lyrics. The end result is a much less pleasing video than the original, with messy editing and showing less of the girls.

DEBUT IN THE WEST

The hottest popstars in the world
right now are t.A.T.u.

The Face Magazine, 2003[51]

On the eve of debuting their first album in the West, Тату's *deus ex machina* decides to step on the gossip and scandal accelerator even harder: an excellent strategy for short distances but often detrimental in the long run. The climax comes during an interview - if you can call it that - of Shapovalov with Tatiana Medvedeva, published[52] on 30th July in the online edition of the renowned Pravda. It is a turbulent meeting in which anything can happen: Shapovalov is assisted by his lawyer, he refuses to answer questions about the girls, attacks the interviewer and eventually provides some arrogant responses:

> Reporter: *As a psychologist, what kind of a relationship do you have with the girls in Tatu?*
>
> Shapovalov: *I am their partner, sexually speaking*
>
> reporter: *Both at the same time?*
>
> Shapovalov: *Yes (laughing)*
>
> Reporter: *Are you instructing them in it?*
>
> Shapovalov: *(laughing) Yes*

On 6th August the news that Lena and Julia are planning a civil union in the Netherlands is reported on NTV.ru (without naming

---

[51] *The Face Magazine,* January 1, 2003.

[52] Tatiana Medvedeva *"ШАПОВАЛОВ СТРОИТ ОТНОШЕНИЯ С "ТАТУ" КАК СЕКСУАЛЬНЫЙ ПАРТНЕР",* Pravda.ru, 30 July 2002.

the source), because same-sex marriage is still not allowed in Russia.

15th August is the official date on which the group's name changes from Тату (or Tatu as reported as the foreign press) to t.A.T.u. From this point on, and starting with the cover of their debut album in English, the characteristic irregular font like a badly-applied rubber stamp and with the 'u' back to front will be used. The official reason is the duplication of name with an Australian group as mentioned before, but it's also rumoured that the change was imposed on Shapovalov by Universal to try to bring about an initial change of course for the duo, who are considered too shocking for the western market[53].

Three days later Lena and Julia start a two-week tour of the USA for the pre-launch of the album and first single in English; among other engagements they do an interview with CNN and pose for many press photo sessions. This is also the first time they meet their new band members.

> When we first met they were shy and didn't speak much English. So it was kinda awkward at first. But then it was just lots of fun. It was really cool when we were with Interscope!. (Troy Maccubbin, 2011)[54]

At their first meeting with the band, the girls do just one rehearsal.
September arrives and t.A.T.u. are popping up all over Europe and the United States whilst the new video for *All The Things She Said* is becoming a big hit on TV music programmes; they arrive in Italy on 5th September to take part in the 'Festivalbar' in Verona. On the Saturday Lena and Julia go on stage dressed in the usual white shirts and ties but with demure blue jeans instead of short skirts, and receive an ovation from the audience. They lip-sync to

---

[53] *Конец Тату*, Sobesednik.ru, 10 August 2002.

[54] troymaccubbin.fanbridge.com, fan questions, 2 May 2011.

All The Things She Said – as practically all the other singers did that year - and as expected they kiss half way through the song. Next day's papers give it plenty of column space, reporting news[55] of a 'shocked audience' and a performance that ended 'in general silence with a few whistles.'

The last night of the summer singing spectacular, which nowadays attracts less interest amongst TV viewers than previously, is recorded as usual for subsequent transmission on Italia 1 in two parts, on the following Tuesday and Saturday. This gives the organisers and broadasting chiefs an opportunity to choose whether to broadcast the kiss sequence or cover the images with shots of the audience. The tendency at first is towards censoring the kiss, but following protests from Arcigay and other organisations the managers of the Mediaset network decide to only partially cover up the contentious images. So the start of the kiss is televised, and then it switches to a wide shot of the Arena for the rest of the kissing sequence. Watching the recording of the performance it's clear that neither during the crucial moment nor afterwards do the audience remain at all silent; in fact they carry on singing and shouting throughout the whole song, although a few whistles can be heard at the end of it.

10th September is the official release date of the single *All The Things She Said* in the USA (it makes its first appearance in the TOP 40 after a month*)*, but Lena and Julia stay in Europe (Spain, Austria, Sweden, the Netherlands, Norway, Czech Republic) to give interviews and meet their fans.

On 16th September *All The Things She Said* goes straight to number 1 on the Italian TOP 20 singles chart, knocking *Asereje* by Las Ketchup from the top spot, and t.A.T.u. are invited to Rome four days later to the open air studio of MTV's 'Total Request Live' in Piazza Argentina where hundreds of fans are expected. Lena and Julia appear in their now classic schoolgirl uniforms and

---

[55] *"Festivalbar non va in tv il bacio delle Tatu"*, Corriere della Sera.it, 9 September 2002.

are given an ironic welcome by the programme presenters who receive them with barely-concealed mockery. After the performance (they lip-sync to *All The Things She Said)*, during which of course Lena and Julia kiss, the presenter Marco Maccarini points out that in his opinion it's better to keep feelings out of performances.

On 3rd October they perform at a concert in Warsaw, Poland in front of a large audience, and the next day Lena celebrates her 18th birthday with the participants of a reality show in Wroclaw (show BAR) at the Polish TV station Polsat which broadcasts the whole event.

In autumn *All The Things She Said* begins to climb the singles charts all over Europe: after going straight to the top in Italy it stays there for four weeks; likewise in Spain. In Italy the album *200 Km/h in the Wrong Lane,* (which in addition to the already-mentioned Russian language tracks contains the cover of *How Soon Is Now* by The Smiths), officially released on 4th October, receives recognition for selling 25,000 copies in a single day, and for 80,000 (a platinum disc) by the end of the year.

But the critics are not always as enthusiastic about t.A.T.u. as the Italian music industry. Marinella Venegoni of La Stampa writes[56] that 'people contaminated by every kind of filth are exploiting those two poor Russian teenagers in t.A.T.u., throwing them up the charts and forcing them to commit acts of lesbianism in front of the miserable TV cameras just to sell records'. And the attitude of condemnation comes not only from the so-called 'adult' press but also from young people's programmes. This is the case with MTV's TRL programme where in October, whilst announcing that *All The Things She Said* has reached number one, the presenters express their disapproval of Lena and Julia's excessive and theatrical

---

[56] Marinella Venegoni *"Novemila persone a Milano per l'unico concerto italiano del «geniettto» di Minneapolis", La Stampa ,* 2 November 2002.

attitude[57]. Even on RAI's weekly Top Of The Pops programme (produced in collaboration with the BBC), the sequences where Lena and Julia kiss are censored before they are shown and covered with shots of the audience[58]. It's clear by now and will become even more so in other countries such as the UK, that western show business will not tolerate the success of the unknown Russian duo and will try to halt their success as much as possible by focussing public attention on the element of scandal rather than on their music.

The conviction that their representatives in Europe (and also in the USA as we find out later) are operating not just under a legitimate doubt as to the authenticity of the girls' uninhibited behaviour in front of the TV cameras, but with actual malicious intent, probably arises from the fact that their music is given less exposure. But the quality of t.A.T.u.'s music cannot be dismissed, however questionable the means of launching it onto the world stage; their way of singing is innovative and captivating, notwithstanding the fact that when they appear on TV they are usually lip-synching (no different from many other acclaimed pop stars) and they are clearly no one hit wonder since their album contains three good hit singles and the rest of the material is of a high quality; and finally, they have the potential to produce at least two more successful albums in the future. If all this is overlooked, which is in fact the case, it reflects deliberate intent to put across the message that it's just a media creation of dubious taste, and not a promising new European pop group.

Fortunately, those who are not distracted by t.A.T.u.'s image but look beyond it and analyse their music can appreciate its quality and originality: musician Greg Rule writes about *200 Km/h in the Wrong Lane* a few months later in Keyboard magazine:

---

[57] *Total Request Live*, MTV Italy, 29 October 2002.

[58] *La RAI censura il video saffico delle Tatu, Gay.it, 4 November 2002.*

> This disc is a piece of Pop perfection [...] their marketing campaign and controversial video for *All The Things She Said* didn't hurt, but I have bought into this disc on sheer pop music power alone (Greg Rule, *Keyboard Magazine*, 2003)

And many other distinguished critics are of the same opinion:

> *All The Things She Said* is an A1, solid gold classic. And, it's not the only gem on this album... musically, pop doesn't get much better than this (Chris Salmon, *Time Out Magazine*, 2003)

> If this is cynical, processed pop, give me some more! because I'm ahamed to say, I think it's totally and utterly fantastic. Here is yet another teenybop act you'd love to loathe but can't because they're so damn talented. (James Delingpole, *The Daily Telegraph*, 2003)

> *200 Km/h in the Wrong Lane* doesn't sound like anything else and I couldn't stop listening (Lisa Verrico, *The Times*, 2003)

The Pop Market Festival is due to take place on 1st November in Tallinn, Estonia. There is much anticipation amongst t.A.T.u. fans there for the only concert at which their favourites are to appear, and when Katina appears alone on stage the audience are dumbfounded. A visibly emotional Lena announces that Julia is ill in hospital in Moscow, and goes on to say, with an apology, that she will only sing *Začem Ja* and *30 Minut*. She sings her own verses of the first song, then at the point in the song where Julia should come in, she stops, quietly asks the audience to sing Julia's parts and bows her head to hide the tears. It's a touching moment, and it's the first occasion where a t.A.T.u. song is performed in public by one of the girls alone, as well as being the first sign of

Julia's health problems that will perhaps be a deciding factor in the group's professional prospects.

On 14th November Lena and Julia - now recovered from her illness - are invited to Barcelona in Spain, to attend the MTV Europe Video Music Awards ceremony as guest stars, where they present Kylie Minogue with the award for best dance singer. t.A.T.u. are not in line for any awards on this occasion, but lip-synch to *All The Things She Said* in the preview show.

The next day Lena and Julia are already in Milan to present the video of their second single, *Not Gonna Get Us* on MTV's TRL, once again as a preview, from the album *200 Km/h in the Wrong Lane*. The girls seem a bit bewildered during the interview and Julia, who is still having problems with her English, barely manages to utter a few words in Russian and leaves almost everything to Lena. She does answer a question from a listener though, who asks them to describe one another using just a few adjectives, and turning to Lena describes her as 'lovely', 'good' and concludes with the statement 'she's mine.' Less confidently, Lena only describes Julia as 'the best'. On every public occasion Julia is the one who appears more determined to portray them as a loving couple, whilst Lena's expressions are more vague.

23rd November is the official release date of the album *200 Km/h in the Wrong Lane* in the United States and Canada, and the girls go to the States to promote it.

The reaction of American critics is perfectly in keeping with t.A.T.u.'s style – mixed. On the one hand they like the Euro-pop sound of their songs, often comparing them to famous predecessors such as ABBA, and on the other hand they hand out a lot of rough criticism of their lyrics in English, their shaky pronunciation and, of course, their image. In December Lena and Julia take part in a number of press and TV interviews in the United States, with shows such as Access Hollywood and Extra.

Towards the end of 2002 persistent rumours begin to circulate about Julia's alleged health problems: the online magazine Express Gazeta[59] reveals on 22nd November that Volkova didn't appear at the concert in Tallin because of problems either with her general health, or with her vocal chords in particular.

During an interview with NTV that goes out on 16th January, Julia admits to having a slight problem with her voice but denies recent reports that she is going to leave the group. A few days later however, t.A.T.u. are forced to announce that the planned one-week stay in London to promote the single *All The Things She Said* in the UK, which is due to be released on January 27, has been cut back to just two days because of Julia's health problems. The next day The Sun newspaper[60] reveals that the treatment Julia is undergoing in Moscow is not having the desired results and the doctors are recommending surgery. The report is partly denied on the 27th on the group's official website: Julia officially has laryngitis and the doctors have suggested surgery, but conventional treatment is working and no operation will be necessary.

These are the first symptoms of what will prove to be for Julia Volkova the biggest problem of her singing career. It is not in fact a simple case of laryngitis, but a cyst on her vocal chords, and it will continue to haunt Julia for years, in spite of treatment. This is the price of the second 'pact with the devil' that the two girls virtually signed, following the one concerning their controversial public image, and inherent in the way of singing that Shapovalov has imposed on them. The high-pitched shrieking, so distinctive and sensual, that make t.A.T.u. songs inimitable are in fact detrimental to the vocal chords of the girls who are no longer children but almost women, and having achieved their success in this way there's no longer any chance of quitting. Emblematic of this is the phrase uttered by Lena a year later when Julia's voice

---

[59] *"Татушка" Юля теряет зрение и голос, "Express Gazeta* 22 November 2002.
[60] *"I'm Tatu ill for UK says Julia» The Sun* , 23 January 2003.

falters in the studio: responding to a member of the team who suggests to Julia that she tries to sing normally, Lena declares: 'our job here is not to sing normally'[61]. To get an idea of the stress that Julia submits her vocal chords to, just listen to the rehearsal for *Not Gonna Get Us* in the Los Angeles studios in 2002[62], where Julia bravely and stoically goes on singing despite her voice giving way as she sings the highest part of the chorus.

Whilst the January 2003 issue of Maxim showing pictures of them in lingerie is still on newsstands in Russia, the public image of Lena and Julia as a lesbian couple starts to crumble towards the end of the month: in Britain the Daily Mail[63], describes them as 'a phenomenon that manages to degrade marketing and music at the same time' and claims to be able to prove that their alleged lesbian relationship is complete fabrication, quoting a statement by Julia's grandmother saying that her granddaughter has a boyfriend who is 'tall and respectable and drives a Mercedes.' A few days later Julia and Lena are exposed by Sunday People[64] photographers at Club B2 in Moscow in the company of their boyfriends Pavel (Pasha) and Mickail. At the time the girls admit to having boyfriends, but then they try to rescue the situation in the following days by saying they are bisexual but prefer women[65]. It has become clear that since t.A.T.u. attained worldwide popularity, defending the lesbian image that helped them reach stardom will not be as easy as it was in the past.

All The Things She Said shoots straight up the UK charts as soon as it is released in February, but in Italy a controversy has blown up at Sanremo Festival. The news has broken that Pippo Baudo has included t.A.T.u. on the list of foreign guests invited to stir up the

---

[61] *t.A.T.u. in Podnebesnaya*, STS TV, Episode 5, 31 January 2004.

[62] *t.A.T.u. Screaming For More* DVD, Interscope, 2004.

[63] Nicole Lampert *"Paedo pop" plumbs the depths"* Daily Mail, 29 January 2003.

[64] Sean O'Brien *"Hot People: Girl-on-girl band Tatu like boys after all ..."* The People, 2 February 2003.

[65] *Tatu-choc: "Siamo bisessuali,"* TGCom24, 10 February 2003.

young audience at the 53rd Festival, and immediately a barrage of politicians, pundits and high-minded people go all out to prevent the scandalous Russian duo from performing on RAI on the opening evening, after what happened a few months earlier at the 'Festivalbar'[66]. Despite Baudo's assurances that good taste will be upheld for the live show, the controversy escalates and only subsides on 28th February[67] when it is officially announced that t.A.T.u. have cancelled, stating problems with one of the girls' vocal chords as the reason.

In the meantime t.A.T.u. have had to fight yet another battle against bigoted conformity in the UK. The BBC had decided[68] not to show the video of *All The Things She Said* in any of their programmes (starting with 'Top Of The Pops') because of the images of the lesbian kiss between the girls. The video (and the kiss) can be seen on British MTV however, which by contrast decided to cut the shots taken from under their skirts, judging them to be indecent. And taking quite a different line, Channel 4's anchorman Richard Madeley had launched a veritable TV crusade to boycott t.A.T.u., accusing their manager Shapovalov of promoting paedophilia[69], and even calling on their record label in the UK, Polydor, to suspend distribution.

On 15th February during the group's stay in the Czech Republic as part of their tour, The Sun publishes and provides evidence[70] of a violent row that has taken place at the Teatrino Hotel in Prague between Julia and Lena, with the latter even having to go to the hospital for stitches in a wound to her leg. The team obviously deny the report of the row, but confirm Lena's injury, claiming it was accidental. On the 18th the group announce the cancellation of

---

[66] Gloria Pozzi, Mario Luzzatto Fegiz '"Tatu", lo scandalo annunciato di Sanremo, *"Corriere della Sera,* 17 February 2003.

[67] "Tatu assenti a Sanremo "Problemi alle corde vocali"," *Corriere della Sera,* 28 February 2003.

[68] Bacio delle T.A.T.U. BBC censura il video, Publiweb.

[69] *"Richard and Judy call for "lesbian single" to be banned,"* the Daily Mail, 1 February 2003.

[70] *"Tatu's Lena in hospital after fight with Julia,"* The Sun , 15 February 2003.

their scheduled concerts in Poland because of the voice problems that Julia is known to be having (dates in Kiev and St. Petersburg have already been cancelled), but in February something even more intimate and personal happens to one of the t.A.T.u. girls: on the 20th the Express Gazeta, always well-informed about the girls' private lives, headlines with 'Tatu Julia has an abortion.'[71] According to the anonymous source cited by the magazine, the voluntary termination of pregnancy took place at a Moscow clinic (the address of which was also supplied) a few days before they left for Prague, and according to the report the news was confirmed on the phone by Julia's mother. They don't link the alleged argument between the girls in Prague with what took place in Moscow a few days earlier.

News of the abortion doesn't get round much at the time and is not officially confirmed until December 2003 when Julia retails the facts in the famous Anatomy of t.A.T.u. documentary, which marks a historic turning point for the group's image, as we shall see later.

> It was a terrible choice. On one hand I had my work: if God decided to make me a star, why should I throw this chance away? But then when I found out I had this tiny being inside me, I was terrified. I cried bitterly at the time. (Julia Volkova, 2003)

Julia celebrates her 18th birthday on February 20 during her stay in Prague, in the days after the abortion. There are no videos of the party that was held for a few close friends at the Selskyi Dvor restaurant, but reports mention a three-tier cake very similar to a wedding cake, with miniature figures of Julia and Lena on top. Shortly after giving Julia the customary kiss, Lena is photographed asleep on the table drunk on wine and bubbly: am image hardly in

---

[71] *"ТАТУШКА" Юля сделала аборт! "Express Gazeta,* February 20, 2003.

keeping with the vulgar, scandalous bad-girl image persistently dragged up by high-minded individuals at the time.

In the second half of February 2003 Mediatraffic[72], which comprehensively analyses sales and radio and TV airings in major countries, puts *All The Things She Said* at the top of the most listened to singles chart, and it stays there for two weeks. Fate is mocking them, and this is one of the signs: at this moment they are the most listened-to group on the planet and a world tour would immediately establish their reputation and bring them considerable financial rewards, but Julia can't sing more than two songs together without losing her voice. On top of that, the original version of *All The Things She Said* has already been out for two years at this point; the protracted length of time between its release in Russia and the rest of the world has taken its toll and is making the lives of Julia and Lena very difficult.

Before the end of February Vanya goes to Los Angeles to prepare for the promotional visit for the album in the United States, and meets PR Robert Hayes. The two put together a plan to shock the American audience, who are deeply concerned about the second Gulf War in Iraq at the time. t.A.T.u. are scheduled to appear on the hugely popular Tonight show with Jay Leno on NBC and need to prepare something that will rouse the attention of the public and the media. Note that talking about Iraq is banned from all entertainment programmes on American networks, so much so that guests have their microphones switched off if they so much as mention a single word about the war. Shapovalov and Hayes decide to get round it by making Lena and Julia wear tee-shirts bearing the slogan 'fucking war' in Russian. On the evening of the show Leno announces his guests and to the tune of *All The Things She Said* Julia and Lena turn to the camera and start singing, displaying the writing on their shirts. And this is not their only defiance: the girls kiss during the live show despite being expressly

---

[72] *Global Track Chart,* Mediatraffic.de, February 22, 2003.

forbidden by the producers, but the director manages to avoid showing the scene by passing quickly to a shot of the band. A reaction from the network is not long awaited: a few days later Globe Magazine announces[73] that t.A.T.u. will never be invited to appear on the Jay Leno show again.

But the plan works, and the following evening Lena and Julia are invited onto the Jimmy Kimmel Show at rival network ABC where they come on wearing tee-shirts bearing the ironic word 'censored.' The interview, in the programme's highly informal style, focuses on the controversy at NBC over censoring the live kiss and the Russian words for 'fucking war' which this time Julia writes on the host's hand in pen.

The initiative is pure tatuism, but in addition to the beneficial media attention that it provokes, however, it also brings t.A.T.u. up against attacks by critics - often fierce attacks. The interview with the NBC programme (coincidence?) 'E! News' a few months later is one example, where the music journalist David Adelson does not hide his disapproval of the attitude of the two singers. To provocative questions such as: 'Are you still counting on spectacular gimmicks or on your music?' Lena tries to respond diplomatically, but Julia intervenes by attacking the presenter and things get heated. At the end of the interview Adelson asks: 'If you become famous superstars, will it change your lives?' and Lena replies ironically: 'We already are superstars.'

> When I look back today at the interviews we gave in America at that time I just think, 'Oh my God!' (Lena Katina, 2013)

In spite of all the adversity they encountered, at the end of the promo-tour in February - the first one with the new band and singing mostly live - t.A.T.u. manage to increase sales of their

---

[73] *Tatu Won't Get Another Invite From Jay Leno,* Popdirt.com, 17 March 2003.

album in the USA and take it from no.189 in the album charts to no.13.

T.A.T.U. AT EUROVISION SONG CONTEST

They return home from the United States on 11th March. Galoyan - who has long since left the band over differences with Vanja[74] - is trying to protect his copyright of *All The Things She Said* against Shapovalov and Neformat[75], and the news begins to circulate that t.A.T.u. might be called on to represent Russia in the 2003 Eurovision Song Contest. The news is bound to cause a stir: t.A.T.u. are currently the most widely-known Russian singers in the world, topping the charts in dozens of countries and adored throughout Europe; they could easily win for Russia, but they're also notorious for being scandalous, unpredictable and having scant regard for diplomacy with the media. Their participation could therefore appear to the staid national TV industries in Europe as provocative and unsuitable for an event that is normally quite sedate, and could earn them more criticism than praise. Also of course, established popstars do tend to eschew singing contests in general, and this one in particular, because the results of the vote are (quite rightly) considered to reflect politico-cultural relationships between participating countries rather than the artistic value of the songs.

Despite all these negative factors Shapovalov is convinced that a victory in the Eurovision Song Contest will raise t.A.T.u.'s profile internationally and most importantly reignite interest in the group

---

[74] Anna Veligzhanina *"Композитор Сергей Галоян:" ТАТУ "СТАЛИ лесбиянками под гипнозом,"* *Komsomolskaya Pravda,* 20 March 2003.
[75] *"I wrote Tatu No.1", The Sun Newspaper,* 5 February 2003.

at home, as it's been more than two years since they launched their first and only album to date.

But for the moment Julia's voice is the main problem: a lot of concerts have been cancelled and the group's management are getting impatient. So a meeting is held at the Neformat headquarters in Moscow[76] involving Lena, Julia, Boris and Vanya, and also the families of the girls and their lawyers. The situation is well known: the cyst that Julia has is still only small but will get bigger over time to the point where surgery is inevitable; the more she uses her voice the quicker the situation will escalate. The problem is, who will take responsibility for deciding what course of action to take: go on with the recordings, performances and concerts as planned, in the hope that the situation remains manageable, or proceed more cautiously as at present. Julia's mother is concerned not just for her daughter's health but also about the financial consequences: the binding contract that the girls (or rather their families) signed at the time commits Julia to reimbursing any financial losses if she unexpectedly becomes unable to continue singing with the group, in effect putting an end to the project. Considering that such losses would be substantial, Julia would lose all the income she has earned up to that point and be left with nothing. But then Vanja objects that singers never remain at the height of popularity for long, and if the girls don't cultivate their success now they will have no popularity left to maintain. 'The artist dies on stage, and Julia, like all artists, gets a fitting reward for her sacrifice,' Vanja proclaims, thus leaving Julia to decide for herself whether to go on or to stop. And it's a difficult decision: each day the programme is delayed costs €200,000 in lost profit and damages, according to Leonid Dzyunik who manages the concerts. At the end of the meeting it's decided to go ahead with the Eurovision Song Contest at least, which for Julia means

---

[76] Vitaly Mansky (director) *АНАТОМИЯ ТАТУ*, STS TV, 12 December 2003.

performing a single song and not the full ninety minutes that a concert would involve.

It is a particularly awkward time for t.A.T.u.: cancellation of their European tour dates in the preceding months has undermined the group's credibility, their scandalous image has been all but dismantled by the press, and those schoolgirl outfits are now starting to feel rather uncomfortable on two eighteen-year-olds. The main driving force behind 'battleship Тату' is starting to stall, and the results are being felt: three UK concerts are cancelled, one of them at Wembley, and the press are quick to speculate that low ticket sales are to blame. Shapovalov, however, declares publicly[77] that the cancellation is down to the British organisers who are afraid of a media boycott of t.A.T.u. in the UK, and the repercussions that would result from the expected attendance of 300 teenagers dressed in school uniform at Wembley for the filming of the new video for *Show Me Love*. The only response the British organisers give is to cite Shapovalov for damages (valued at around €500,000) for cancellation of the three concerts[78], but since the organisers claim that the concerts have been cancelled due to Julia's inability to sing, Vanja shrewdly brings the girls with him to London the day before the date scheduled for the performance and has them declare to the press that they are ready to perform at any time.

Shortly afterwards the promo-tour in Japan is cancelled and a rumour about some crisis between Lena and Julia starts to spread[79]. An eleventh-hour attempt is launched to rescue the girls' public image, which this time involves Lena rekindling an idea that was exploited before, of a civil partnership in Germany with Julia after

---

[77] Yuri Yarotskaya *Их не раскупишь Kommersant.ru* no.76, 5 May 2003.
[78] *Lawsuit over Tatu cancellations,* BBC News Online, 1 May 2003.
[79] Anna Tioková *"Начало конца," Gala* no.5, May 2003.

the hoped-for victory at Eurovision, which she broaches in an interview with an online magazine[80].

Shapovalov, however, continues to show confidence and decides to proceed as planned in early May with the filming of the new video - which is due to take place after London in Moscow, New York (later moved to Los Angeles) and Tokyo - and through announcements made on MTV manages to gather together dozens of sixteen-year-olds all wearing miniskirts, blouses and ties on Westminster Bridge in London, not far from the Houses of Parliament. But once again the UK demonstrates that it is no great ally of t.A.T.u.: the police refuse permission to film on the grounds of public order, and because insufficient notice is given in advance[81]. So the filming is done with girls recruited from a modelling agency in another, less well-known part of the city and away from official premises on the top of a double decker bus, in order to circumvent the ban imposed by the authorities on entry into the city.

On May 15, just days before leaving for the Eurovision Song Contest, Shapovalov has no better luck at home. The venue chosen for the shoot in Moscow is Red Square, where Vanya brings together hundreds of girls in school uniform, but filming is quickly blocked by the police[82]. Lena and Julia are filmed by TV cameras being bundled into a police car, smiling. The girls are transferred by coach to another area (where a few scenes are filmed surreptitiously) and Shapovalov is taken first to Kitay-Gorod police station and then straight to court[83]. Vanja had not actually been given permission to shoot in the famous square which, by virtue of an old law that has never been repealed is still a strategic target and subject to stringent restrictions, but he hoped to avoid

---

[80] *"Tatu plan to wed"*, Contactmusic, 2 May 2003.

[81] *"Police do not take too kindly to 100 teenage girls dressed in school uniform causing an obstruction,"* New Musical Express, 7 May 2003.

[82] *"Tatu Barred From Filming Video»* Contactmusic, 15 May 2003

[83] *"Tatu manager arrested during the video shoot,"* New Musical Express, 16 May 2003.

problems with the excuse of having intended to film the official promo video for Eurovision at the same time.

The next day, on the eve of t.A.T.u.'s departure for the Eurovision Song Contest, the long-awaited press conference is held in a room at the Izvestia media centre[84], which is crowded with Russian and international journalists and cameramen.

Yulri Aksyuta on behalf of the Channel One Russia TV station confirms that the regulations for the event have been observed, that t.A.T.u. have been chosen after hearing several other candidates in the preselection, and that the group indeed represents the biggest music ensemble in Russia and is therefore the most likely to secure victory. The international journalists of course home in on Shapovalov, asking if there will be any scandals at Eurovision, but Vanja replies with irony that he has never had any intention of shocking anyone in any way. Shapovalov then officially announces his plan[85] to take the band's backing vocalist, Katya Nechaeva, to Riga, where the festival is being held: it is not yet clear whether the jury will admit the use of recorded backing vocals, and if not the vocalist will support Lena and (especially) Julia live on stage.

Seventeen-year-old Nechaeva, whose voice has already featured as backing vocal on a few of t.A.T.u.'s recorded tracks, has been targetted in press reports in recent days: Julia's well-chronicled problems with her vocal chords are worrying not only for the group's management but also for Channel One bosses who fear that t.A.T.u. might let Russia down in front of 150 million spectators if Volkova's voice fails in the middle of the live performance at the Festival. For this reason the press have begun to refer to the young girl, who looks a lot like Julia, as 'the third t.A.T.u.'

The choice of original song for the festival, *Ne Ver', Ne Boysia*, is fast-paced and aggressive: attractive to a youthful audience but not quite in line with the traditional aplomb of the festival. The

---

[84] *"ТАТУ НИКОГО НЕ ХОТЯТ ПОБЕДИТЬ,"* Izvestia, 18 May 2003.

[85] *"Tatu introduces third member,"* Contactmusic, 21 May 2003.

Russian lyrics will also have to be toned down to avoid censorship problems. The title (originally *Ne Ver', Ne Boysia, Ne Prosi)* references the three commandments of prisoners in the gulag, 'do not believe, do not fear, do not ask,' immortalised by Aleksandr Solzhenitsyn in the 70s, and also in Varlam Shalamov's *Kolyma Tales*[86].

In Riga fears for Julia's voice grow: the girl has difficulty singing and her voice is showing signs of stress after only a few minutes. On top of that, t.A.T.u. are cited as favourites in the European press, and some scandal or other is expected from them during the show, which is aimed at family viewing. The atmosphere is tense and everyone is poised for total catastrophe and chaos in the usual t.A.T.u. style, which is exactly what happens.

The first dress rehearsal is, to say the least, disastrous: Julia cannot sing, the lights are positioned in such a way that the girls are in shadow when they move around the stage, and the atmosphere is particularly hostile, so much so that Julia decides to abandon the session, walking off the stage to the general exasperation of everyone present. At the next rehearsal a few hours later Lena appears on her own. At this point t.A.T.u. are even refusing to talk to the press, except for public press conferences organised by the festival.

The organisers are aware from t.A.T.u.'s reputation that the girls are capable of disregarding all agreements put in place before the event once they're on stage, and it causes them so much anxiety that they announce several days in advance[87] that they're poised to switch to a broadcast of one of their recorded rehearsals at any moment if Lena and Julia's behaviour on stage goes too far. But after the way things have been going, the director has no complete recording of any dress rehearsal at that point, and t.A.T.u. are

---

[86] Varlam Šalamov, *Kolyma Tales*, Adelphi Ed. 1995.

[87] *"Tatu fear for Eurovision," Contactmusic*, 20 May 2003.

warned that they must attend the final scheduled rehearsals (one of them in costume) under penalty of disqualification.

What the organisers don't know (officially Julia is just suffering from laryngitis) is that Julia's voice is now in the worst condition it's ever been and could fail at any moment. Vanja decides to consult a doctor to get a certificate allowing her to sing as little as possible and skip the three scheduled rehearsals (two on the eve of the competition and one in costume the following day, shortly before the broadcast). The event organisers are of course opposed to this, but a compromise is reached whereby Lena will attend the remaining rehearsals alone, whilst Julia undergoes 32 hours of inhalation therapy and maintains absolute silence. Julia's absence at the dress rehearsal on the Saturday is one of the detrimental factors that affect t.A.T.u.'s final placement: the technical juries of a number of countries, amongst them Ireland, make their judgements based on the performance in this final round where Lena sings alone (Nechaeva provides back-up but is not front of stage), which is heavily booed by the live audience. Lena comes out at the end of the rehearsal clearly annoyed and saying, 'it's all over.'

Julia arrives a few hours later and the girls dress very simply for the show: jeans, trainers and two white tee-shirts each with a big number 1 on the front (the judges have rated their song number 11). Their performance is shaky at the start: as well as nerves, Lena's pitch in the first verse leaves a lot to be desired, and the TV cameras take mainly long-distance shots of the girls, probably because their failure to complete any rehearsals has given the director no chance of preparing any edited shots (or perhaps to avoid broadcasting any mood changes). Despite initial setbacks however, Lena and Julia are confident and put everything into their performance. The reaction of the hundreds of young people in the audience, many of them fans of t.A.T.u., is encouraging, and at the end of the performance they exit to applause from the public.

Backstage, Julia is over the moon with the performance: everyone was expecting a debacle, and instead everything (or almost everything) went according to plan. The girls are mobbed by journalists but they're exhausted and take refuge in a private area without making any comment. Once the adrenaline rush has died away Julia and Lena appear smiling on the direct link with Russian TV; Julia complains about the sound, starting with the voice echo which was set too low, and Lena points out that the shots of them were too wide and there were no close-ups, suggesting that it was all done deliberately to avoid broadcasting them kissing. Both of them had the impression that they were deliberately disadvantaged to penalise Russia in the final stakes, but they're still convinced they can win.

When voting starts it immediately becomes clear that winning the top spot will not be easy. Belgium and Turkey are at the top of the leaderboard after the first votes are announced, and t.A.T.u. are relegated to third place. Votes from the UK and Ireland are announced next, with 0 points for Russia: a crushing blow. The whole team are heavily disappointed: the concert manager hotly declares:

> There was no song, there was no show and we told all the journalists to go to hell . And that's what we get. (Leonid Dzyunik, 2003)

Shapovalov, who had made himself scarce during the voting, speaks to the press more calmly[88]:

> We did not come here to win first place, although we always had the potential to win. We wanted to sacrifice ourselves for our country, we wanted to transform our love for our homeland into votes for Russia, but it was not enough. (Ivan Shapovalov, 2003)

---

[88] *"Иван Шаповалов комментирует итоги" Евровидения "*, *Intermedia*, 25 May 2003.

But Vanja doesn't shrink from implicating the organisers too, accusing them of somewhat stonewalling the girls because they feared some kind of improper behaviour from them on stage.

In the days that follow tatuism levels reach a peak: in an audit of the vote-counting it transpires that Ireland did not take into account the public vote (votes phoned in by TV viewers), and judging was calculated entirely on votes from the technical jury based on the disastrous dress rehearsal where Lena sang on her own. According to calculations by Channel One Russia, if the public vote had been taken into account in Ireland, t.A.T.u. would have won first place[89] since there were only three votes between the winner, Turkey, and Russia who came third. The EBU which organises the festival replies in an official letter to the Russian broadcasters that the public vote in Ireland was not taken into account due to a problem with the telephone company which was late in transferring the data, and which was given orally just one minute before they went on air, so the decision was taken to disregard it. The debate goes on in the press for a few days, but it's clear that the official result of the competition will remain unchanged; however, a year after the affair, as revealed by Julia in 2012[90], the EBU send a formal letter to Channel One Russia assigning first place to t.A.T.u. following a recount of the votes.

What happened at Eurovision is a reflection of much of t.A.T.u.'s history: contentious relations with the press and the authorities, managers that are often arrogant, hostile behaviour towards foreign organisers, chronic unreliability and a large share of bad luck. But in spite of all these negative external influences, Lena and Julia - who are now 'the biggest pop sensation on the planet' according to the Sydney Morning Herald[91] - manage to make their mark on the

[89] Первый канал получил доказательства подтасовки результатов голосования на "Евровидении", News.ru, 27 May 2003.
[90] "ТАТУ" признали победителями Евровидения, Siteua.org, 15 December 2012.
[91] Neil McCormick "Tatu's company", Sydney Morning Herald, 24 May 2003.

history of global pop music and stay close to the hearts of millions of fans for more than ten years; this would not be the case if t.A.T.u. were simply what their image suggests: a couple of excitable and rebellious lesbian teenagers (ex-teenagers by this stage) who were thrust into the limelight, because that initial powerful image that steered 'battleship Тату' to success is now in the process of being dismantled for good.

T.A.T.U.'S INVERSE COMING OUT

When the fallout from their defeat at Eurovision is over t. A.T.u. have to try to revive their international popularity, and on 31st May they're in Los Angeles as guests at the MTV Movie Awards. *All The Things She Said* is playing as Julia and Lena enter the stage alone, and they are joined shortly after by almost two hundred girls in school uniform who sing *Not Gonna Get Us* live, along with them. It's an exciting show and reaches its climax when the girls all rip off their skirts revealing chaste white knickers, and kiss. For the first time the scandal is enacted *around* Lena and Julia and not *by* them, although pictures of them kissing and gossip articles about their relationship are projected onto the background. Their vocal performance is not the best: Julia has trouble singing in spite of the mass of backing vocals, and even Lena seems a bit out of breath, but they get a heartfelt ovation from the crowd.

As far as concerts are concerned things are not going so well: the t.A.T.u. management in its usual style cancels the concert at Kipsala Arena in Riga at the last minute, when more than 80% of the tickets have already been sold[92]. The group's failure to observe their contractual obligations this time provokes a reaction from the local organisers (the group are still keeping quiet about Julia's voice problems which mean she can't sing for the duration of an entire concert), and Neformat are sued for damages[93].

The same happens with their next date, scheduled for June 14 in Turkey, which is cancelled for no apparent reason. The Turkish

---

[92] *Концерт "Тату" в Риге отменен*, DELPHI, 9 June 2003.
[93] *Par line atcelto "Tatu" koncertu vērsīsies tiesa*, TVNet, 11 June 2003.

press interpret the cancellation as revenge for the contested Eurovision result.

Shapovalov and his colleagues are more creative when they have to justify cancelling three shows in Israel (subsequently reduced to a single date in Tel Aviv, as ticket sales are also insufficient): it's announced that the Israeli authorities have not granted entry visas so Julia and Lena are unable to travel to Tel Aviv. The deception is exposed[94] by the press office of the Israeli Ministry of the Interior: the visas for t.A.T.u. were dispatched more than 10 days previously and the local organisers were well aware of it.

Putting aside the controversies over cancellations for the moment, t.A.T.u.'s management now focuses on the forthcoming trip to Japan to promote the album, and also to shoot some more scenes for the problematic *Show Me Love* video. Following a 'call to arms' by Shapovalov similar to those in London and Moscow where several hundred young girls aged between 16 and 25 are asked to attend, the headquarters of Universal KK (the Japanese subsidiary of Universal) receive in excess of 35,000 applications from young Japanese girls hoping to take part in the video alongside t.A.T.u. But not even the Land of the Rising Sun is prepared to allow Shapovalov to go ahead unchallenged with his giant harem: according to the local press, police in many districts of the city (Shapovalov has not disclosed where the filming will take place) are in a state of pre-alert to stop t.A.T.u. and their management if they become a threat to public order[95].

And as expected, a few hours before the shoot scheduled for 29th June in the shopping districts of Akihabara and Ginza, the Tokyo authorities refuse Shapovalov's request for authorisation. It is significant that this time Universal Music KK officially announce that they are not directly involved in the production of the video.

---

[94] *"ТАТУ": новые подробности скандала*, DNI.ru, 19 June 2003.
[95] *Японские власти угрожают "ТАТУ"*, Music.com.ua, 26 June 2003.

It is not known if this clarification from the recording company is because company bosses are exasperated with general problems arising from Vanja's delusions of grandeur, or if there are other sources of disagreement with him. In any case, nerves become frayed the next evening whilst t.A.T.u. are actually at the studios of the Japanese TV station Asahi, waiting their turn to appear on the live 'Music Station' programme for which they have already done rehearsals and in which their participation has been announced. Following a frantic phonecall from Vanja (who is not present at the studios) Leonid tells the girls disappointedly that they've been ordered to leave the studio and abandon the broadcast.

> Leonid begged us, saying, 'girls, don't pay any attention to him, don't give up the broadcast.' But we were so young; Ivan was the one who'd done everything for us and made us successful: how could we not listen to him? (Lena Katina, 2013)

The music channel receives dozens of phone calls in protest from disappointed viewers who were looking forward to Lena and Julia's performance. Shapovalov also decides to cancel a performance scheduled at a venue in Tokyo where more than a thousand fans are waiting for the girls. In this case Universal also add their own apology[96].

At a crowded press conference on June 29, two days after the events at Asahi TV, Shapovalov explains that the girls did not feel comfortable being in the studio alongside a great many Japanese stars: t.A.T.u. should have been performing alone as was expressly requested, but there had obviously been problems with communication. In an interview with the program 'Bankisha' on NTV Julia states that the decision to abandon the broadcast was taken independently by Vanja, who was probably watching the live

---

[96] *"Russian pop duo Tatu cancels two performances in Japan as troubles mount", Europe Intelligence Wire*, 28 June 2003.

broadcast in his hotel room, and that she and Lena were against the decision.

The day after their departure the Tokyo tabloids have nothing good to say about t.A.T.u.[97], who at their last press conference in Tokyo said they'd actually enjoyed their time in Japan and that they were sure they'd managed to increase their fanbase there.

Years later, Lena reflects that this incident probably marked the beginning of their boss's egocentric tendencies:

> Everything started with the trip to Japan. Someone just overestimated his importance. And ours as well. He was going mad. (Lena Katina, 2012)[98]

This is without a doubt the worst of t.A.T.u.'s early troubles: last-minute cancellations, disputes with the authorities and the press, arguments with record companies, TV broadcasters and concert organisers. t.A.T.u. - or rather their management - it seems, can make enemies everywhere they go. And this is demonstrated once again in August at the National Dance Music Awards 'Dvizhenie-2003' sponsored by the Intermedia agency (the major source of music industry communications in Russia) which is due to award the prize for most successful pop group of the year. t.A.T.u. are declared the winners, but Shapovalov decides to disregard the awards ceremony entirely: news reports[99] quote Shapovalov's spiteful retort: 'To hell with them and their prizes: they should have thought of us before, when we weren't so famous in Europe.'

Returning to Moscow on August 14 after a t.A.T.u. concert in Turkey, Julia suddenly complains of severe pain in her appendix; she requires immediate hospitalisation and an emergency operation

---

[97] *"No gain for Tatu in Tokyo but they vow to come back"*, Europe Intelligence Wire, 30 June 2003.

[98] Eugene Levkovich, *"Площадь Ленина"*, Rolling Stone Magazine Russia, June 2012.

[99] *"Группа ТАТУ отказалась от Движения"*, Komsomolskaya Pravda, 13 August 2003.

to avoid peritonitis. The operation is a success, and Julia's concerns about the scar also prove to be unfounded.

The following evening t.A.T.u. are scheduled to play at the renowned VIVA Comet Awards in Cologne, and for the second time in less than a year Lena is once again alone on stage in front of thousands of youngsters. She manages by lip-synching to *Not Gonna Get Us* and urging the audience to sing Julia's parts in her absence.

The legal battle between Elena Kiper and her former partner Shapovalov and Neformat commences in September 2003[100]. Kiper claims copyright for the tracks *Ya Soshla S Uma* (and therefore also *All the Things She Said)* and *Nas Ne Dogonyat* (and likewise *Not Gonna Get Us*). If Kiper were to win the civil cause, she could demand suspension of sales of the albums containing the tracks, the production of the CD, broadcasts on radio and TV and performance of the songs at t.A.T.u. concerts. Shapovalov, who does not attend the initial hearing claiming he didn't receive notification, declares publicly that he can't understand the reason for the lawsuit when it's four years since the songs were written[101].

Meanwhile, as Lena and Julia announce that they'll be taking separate holidays in late September, two events crucial for t.A.T.u.'s future appear on the horizon.

The first is a documentary about Lena and Julia that director and journalist Vitaly Mansky announces himself to be on the verge of completing. Mansky, who is well known in Russia for his documentaries on the lives of Mikhail Gorbachev, Boris Yeltsin and Vladimir Putin, says in an interview with the Lithuanian Telegraph newspaper that because of the content and the language used the documentary may not be broadcast on television, but will be released as a DVD later that year.

---

[100] *"Группа" ТАТУ "останется без хитов?" Komsomolskaya Pravda*, 9 September 2003.
[101] *"'ТАТУ" СКРЫВАЮТ АВТОРОВ НОВЫХ ПЕСЕН", Intermedia*, 16 September 2003.

The second event is announced to a crowded press conference in the penthouse of the Peking Hotel in Moscow by the Shapovalov himself: t.A.T.u. are about to start recording their new album and all the recording sessions will be filmed by the cameras for a reality show to be aired on Russian TV. Even backstage footage from two mega-concerts at the giant 40,000-seat Tokyo Dome in Japan on 1st and 2nd December will be included in the TV show.

Lena and Julia's complex personal relationship seems to be going through a crisis at this time. After spending their two-week holiday apart in September, Julia isn't even with Lena for her 19th birthday party on October 4. When asked about Julia's whereabouts, Lena replies with beautiful melancholic blue eyes that 'she wished me happy birthday this morning on the phone.[102]'

In mid-October it's officially announced that t.A.T.u. will be winners at the World Music Awards in Montecarlo in three categories: World's Best Pop Group, World's Best Duet and World's Best Dance Group. It's an event that t.A.T.u. attend every year; a charity event, rubbing shoulders with singers, actors, VIPs and members of the Monaco royal family, and this time Shapovalov plans to shake up the dignified proceedings by sending Lena and Julia on stage armed with real submachine guns loaded with blanks. The organisers obviously refuse and supply the girls with plastic machine guns instead. The girls think it's ridiculous to go on stage with plastic guns, and with Vanja's approbation they decide to boycott the ceremony and stay in their luxury hotel on the evening of the event.

In November comes another of Shapovalov's sensationalistic ideas to provoke the world of music show business: t.A.T.u. are again nominated for the prize of best Russian artists of the year at the MTV European Music Awards, which they also won in 2001, but the group announce their intention to hand their votes over to their friends in the group Leningrad to give them a chance to win.

---

[102] *День рождения Лены без Юли,* Dni.ru, 7 October 2003.

Naturally, the panel of judges opposes this unusual transfer of preferences.

On 25th October following a performance in Hong Kong, Lena and Julia return to Japan to promote two major concerts scheduled in Tokyo on the first two days of December, as part of the new *Show Me Love* Tour. t.A.T.u.'s popularity is off the scale in Japan by now, so much so that the Japanese branch of Universal launched a maxi-single a few months earlier with a cover of *All The Things She Said* sung in Japanese by two seventeen year olds, Emi Suzuki and Juria Oki, under the name of Juemilia.

When they arrive at Marita airport the girls appear exhausted and scuffles break out between their personal bodyguards and Japanese journalists who are pushing for an interview or just a photograph. After their official commitments, including a meeting with the Japanese sponsors of the two forthcoming shows, Lena returns to Moscow alone whilst Julia and Vanja spend two more days in Tokyo shopping.

On 8th November rumours appear in the Japanese daily, Fuji Evening News, which claim that tickets sales for the two t.A.T.u. concerts are much lower than the sponsors expected, possibly because of the high price (7,500 Yen: about $75 US). According to the newspaper, only 30,000 of the 90,000 tickets available have been sold for the two concerts with a little under a month to go. The newspaper conjectures that this must be annoying for the sponsors, as official commentators say t.A.T.u. will have to receive a total of 300 million Yen as compensation ($3 million).

Distribution of the DVD *Screaming for More* is now launched through Amazon in the UK; it contains all the official videos so far released in Russian and English, as well as a few behind-the-scenes rehearsals, photos and a previously unreleased version of *All The Things She Said* in Dolby Surround 5.1

On 12th November Lena and Julia each go separately (to avoid recognition) to see a concert in Moscow by SMASH!, a pop duo formed of Vlad Topalov and Serguey Lazarev, two boys roughly the same age as the girls who they know from Neposedi. The girls are recognised by their friends and are invited on stage where they improvise a song with them. Three years later the press claim that Topalov is in a relationship with Julia[103].

On 28th November Shapovalov officially announces that t.A.T.u. will be working on their next album in early 2004, accompanied by TV cameras in a sort of reality show by the title of 'Podnebesnaya' (Under the Sky), to be broadcast on the STS television network. The shooting will take place in a specially designed TV studio on the thirteenth floor of the Peking Hotel in Moscow, inside the clock tower (Podnebesnaya is coincidentally also the old name for China). As part of the show Shapovalov and the group will choose a new song from ones sent in by amateur composers.

What the public don't know is that Vanya is in fact in big trouble at the moment: his existing contract with Universal includes production of t.A.T.u.'s second album in early 2004, but all the creative people (Alex, Sergio, Elena) who collaborated to produce *200 Po Vstrechnoy* have long since walked out, and no decent replacements have been found. So it looks like he won't be able to put together any tracks for the album. Boris Rensky tries to cut their losses by contacting Galoyan again, and he agrees to come back and work on the project, but only on condition that Vanya is out of it. Both Rensky and the girls have suspected for some time that Shapovalov will be the death of t.A.T.u. and the confirmation comes soon enough.

The date of the first concert at the Tokyo Dome comes round. Julia is suffering from the flu; she has a fever and is unable to eat much or keep anything down, so they skip rehearsals for the show; another major problem here too though, seems to be Vanya's relationship with the local organisers. The Japanese are unwilling to delegate control of the show to Shapovalov and he is even

---

[103] *"Сенсация: Юля встречается с Владом Топаловым!", BRAVO! Russia* no.17, April 2006.

banned from joining the girls backstage. Vanya threatens to cancel the show, and whilst negotiations are going on more than 25,000 youngsters have to wait in the auditorium for almost an hour with no information. Eventually Lena, Julia and the director of Neformat, Sergey Bobza, join Shapovalov outside the building, and after a few minutes' conversation they decide to start the show, which will be shortened, however, because of the delay and because of Julia's uncertain state of health. Dozens of Japanese girls dressed in school uniform go on stage with t.A.T.u.; they've been selected in advance from amongst the group's fans to take part in a few dance routines, practised beforehand. Shapovalov manages to gain control of the second show.

Two such enormous concerts within twenty four hours of each other prove too much even for Lena, who appears very tired on stage during the second show and passes out backstage at the end. Lena recovers with Julia's assistance and the whole episode is recorded by the STS TV cameras and used some time later in the reality show 't.A.T.u. in Podnebesnaya'. Julia attributes the incident partly to the stress of doing a double show and partly to Lena's diet: she is eating very little at this time to keep her figure slender as befits their image. Many tickets remain unsold (a little under half of those available), but t.A.T.u.'s management say they're satisfied with the concerts, explaining that they didn't expect to fill all the 40,000 seats in the Tokyo Dome on both nights, and that the Monday and Tuesday dates were not convenient for the group's young fans to attend.

t.A.T.u. are in fact extremely popular in Japan, so much so that Shapovalov's plans even include a cartoon film starring the animated alter egos of Julia and Lena. Vanja makes contact with well-known filmmakers Shinichiro Watanabe for the opening and Norio Kashima and Susumu Kudo for the film itself, and calls the project 't.A.T.u. Paragate'. because Julia and Lena's animated personae are meant to have something to do with a portal into the paranormal. In 2003 the website goes online promising release in the winter of 2004, and the merchandising is presented at the 65th Comic Market in Tokyo. But an unexpected split between t.A.T.u. and Shapovalov brings the project to a premature end and the website closes down in 2005.

Vitaly Mansky's documentary 'Anatomy of t.A.T.u.' finally goes out on STS network's main TV channel on the evening of December 12. The documentary film causes an immediate uproar amongst fans: Julia and Lena are shown in their private life, revealing that they have habits that no-one really suspected before, such as smoking - extremely bad practice for professional singers - and one of them (Julia) even confesses to having used drugs. Lena incredibly turns out to be very shy and a devout Orthodox Christian, whilst Julia seems more open-minded and up for anything just to achieve and maintain success. The severity of the condition of Julia's voice is revealed, and the fact that t.A.T.u. were close to being dissolved because of it. But the biggest revelation in the documentary is the couple's inverse coming out: Lena and Julia are not lesbians at all and never have been, and when she's off-scene Julia is constantly with her boyfriend Pasha. The lesbian relationship between the two was an invention of Shapovalov's to trigger media interest, and Lena has been finding it difficult all this time to act it out in front of the TV cameras. The reason the girls have decided to now uncover the hoax is clear: Shapovalov has become uncontrollable and they need a radical change. The numerous t.A.T.u. forums register a variety of reactions from fans bewildered by Lena's confession, but as Lena recalls today, she avoids reading them:

> In the very early days I used to follow everything the fans wrote about us and reacted emotionally, but I soon realised there was no point in doing that because there would always be opinions for and against, and anyway, the rational intelligent people

around me knew how it really was and why I did the things I did, so I just stopped reading them. (Lena Katina, 2013)

18th December is to be Lena & Julia's first concert following the revelations made in the 'Anatomy of t.A.T.u.' documentary, and it is eagerly awaited. 18,000 fans flock to the concert in St. Petersburg, taking advantage of the particularly low ticket price of only 3 dollars, and tragedy is narrowly avoided on a number of occasions because there are insufficient security measures in place: many young people pass out, crushed against the barriers by the crowd, and a lot of scuffles break out before the concert begins. The expectations of the audience are not disappointed: Lena and Julia embrace, caress and kiss each other on stage as usual. Apparently nothing has changed since their inverse coming-out a few days ago. But has nothing really changed?

FAREWELL TO SHAPOVALOV

On 8th January 2004 the Swedish magazine Aftonbladet[104] announces that Lena Katina intends to leave t.A.T.u. In an exclusive interview with reporters Bäck and Petersson, according to the magazine, she expresses all the frustration that's built up from having to do Shapovalov's bidding for the last four years and pretend to be a lesbian. She also reveals that she and Julia can no longer stand each other, citing as an example her partner's cold, brief phone call to wish her a happy 19th birthday a few months back instead of coming to the small family party that was organised, which upset her enormously. Lena adds that she has received offers from the United States and that she wishes to pursue a solo career.

This bombshell is repeated in many European newspapers, including The Sun[105], but raises a lot of doubt: it seems odd that Katina has decided to disclose this important decision to a Swedish newspaper and not in her own country, and only a few days before the new reality TV show.

Something is definitely going on, that much is obvious; on the eve of his departure Vanja now wants to demonstrate that he's the one calling the shots, so when journalist Anna Kovaleva of Izvestia[106] asks him when the t.A.T.u. project will be ending, he remarks arrogantly: 'When I decide.'

---

[104] Bertil Bäck, Claes Petersson *"Jag vill inte stripping lesbisk", Aftonbladet*, 8 January 2004.
[105] *"Tatu: We arent lesbians", The Sun Newspaper,* 9 January 2004.
[106] *"Иван Шаповалов: Не хватает любви ", Izvestia,* 16 January 2004.

The first episode of 't.A.T.u. in Podnebesnaya' is broadcast on Saturday 17 January on the STS network. t.A.T.u. fans are disappointed[107]: the TV cameras show Shapovalov engrossed in cerebral conversations on show business matters and about the future of t.A.T.u. with some guests, and this goes on for forty minutes. Julia and Lena only appear in the last few minutes of the programme, in a clip recorded in November when they were arguing with photographer Vladimir Kovalyuk and messing up the shoot for the programme's official picture. No reference is made to the recording of the new album, which was supposed to be the main topic of the show according to what was announced. The day after, a brief advert on the network announces that recording of the new t.A.T.u. album as part of 'Podnebesnaya' is suspended, and on the Sunday evening instead of the advertised second episode, a repeat of the 'Anatomy of t.A.T.u.' documentary is shown.

It's clear that something major occurred the day after the first episode was broadcast, and it all comes out in the next episode on January 24. Lena and Julia state in front of the TV cameras that they are deeply disappointed with what went out the week before: it should have been a reality show about t.A.T.u. and instead it was turned into some sort of monologue by Shapovalov, who is becoming more and more egocentric. In a conversation with her family Lena gives the impression that the bond of trust with Vanja is broken:

I've been working with him several years now and I see him getting worse every day. The situation is already out of control, we've crossed the line and there's no going back [...] I respect him for what he did, but I don't respect him for what he's doing now, I'm disappointed in him as a person, as an individual.

---

[107] *"А были ли девочки?"*, *Komsomolskaya Pravda*, 19 January 2004.

Julia too points out how insensitive Vanja has been with regard to her voice problems, which are well-known:

He doesn't care what happens to my voice, he doesn't give a damn... He just says, 'Oh, so you can't sing anymore, well that's it for you then, we'll find someone else. Either you sing today or someone else will sing tomorrow.'

Then it comes out that, contrary to what Shapovalov was claiming up till the day before, the songs for the album are not ready at all; in fact they have nothing to record and the March deadline that the 2003 contract with Universal Russia stipulates cannot be met. The record label is obviously already aware of the fact that the album will not be ready in time and decides to release an album of remixes containing the Eurovision entry *Ne Ver, Ne Boisya* for the first time, to maintain interest in the group after more than a year with no new releases.

The reality show is suspended and broadcasting continues for several episodes with material recorded in 2003 ranging from behind-the-scenes footage of the Tokyo concerts to the events at Eurovision, alternated with some dull studio rehearsals recorded between 2003 and 2004 of boring songs chosen by Shapovalov with lyrics about war and politics - nothing like the style of t.A.T.u.'s other songs. Ratings plummet and yet again Vanja tries to play the scandal card:

I've often said in public that I like children, and Vanya had the idea of putting out a false report that I was expecting a baby whilst the show was going out. He even wanted me to wear padding to make it look like my belly was growing. I told him it was out of the question, and ironically soon after that Julia told us she really was pregnant. (Lena Katina, 2013)

Julia knew it wasn't the best time for her to be pregnant. The press[108] find out much later that Volkova had been to a specialist clinic in Moscow in February to see about having an abortion, like she did the year before. But this time Julia is in her sixth week and she's not in the best state of health generally, so the answer from the doctors is not favourable: an interruption of the pregnancy would probably leave her sterile. A few months later, in the documentary 'Ta-Ta Tatu?'[109], Lena tells how Julia consulted her about it even before she told her family, and that she advised her to definitely keep the baby.

But the most interesting thing that comes out of the episodes broadcast in March are the reports of clashes between Julia and Vanja over the way she uses her voice. These clashes took place in January - so before the controversies of the 24th and before the pregnancy. Volkova refuses to do the high-pitched screeching that she did on the first album, but Shapovalov insists on sticking to the same formula, saying 'without the screeching at the beginning and end of the song, it will never take off.' In January it turns out that Julia's voice problems are back, and doctors warn her against putting too much strain on it, so the girl is obliged to produce a medical certificate to convince Vanya to stop rehearsals. Shapovalov tries to get Lena to sing Julia's parts, but her voice doesn't have the same pitch as Volkova's so it doesn't work. During this period the backing singer Nechaeva makes regular appearances on Podnebesnaya.

The relationship between t.A.T.u. and their *deus ex machina* is irreparably broken: on February 6 lawyer Audrey Yakovlev notifies Shapovalov of the mandate she has received from her clients, Lena Katina and Julia Volkova, to terminate the contract with Neformat for breach of the latter. The non-compliances that the lawyer cites are failure to sign a new deal with Universal Music

---

[108] *" ТАТУШКА" хотела избавиться от ребенка ", Zhizn,* May 22, 2004.
[109] *"Ta-Ta Tatu?", Russian Hour,* 20 September 2004.

for a more appropriate distribution of t.A.T.u. records, and non-payment of the singers' entitlements for records sold, for which Neformat have never even provided official estimates to the artists. Shapovalov's immediate reaction is immortalised by the Podnebesnaya cameras. Vanja doesn't seem particularly surprised or angry; with his usual aplomb, and probably confident of regaining control of the situation quite easily, he calls Lena to ask her to come to the studio for a recording (Julia does not answer when he calls). Lena is amazed that he can ask her to do such a thing as if nothing has happened, and obviously reiterates what's in the documents, telling him that she stands by them. There are probably a few people there in the studio with Vanja who can see exactly what the outcome of this paradoxical situation will mean: the bond of dependence and affection that existed between Vanja and the girls is now broken, and without that bond t.A.T.u. will be artistically barren and no longer able to produce anything worthwhile.

Vanja also reveals that six months earlier, when they were in Los Angeles, he had suggested to Lena and Julia that they terminate the t.A.T.u. project: one album, a triumph, and then end it. But on that occasion it was mutually agreed to continue.

The next episodes of 'Podnebesnaya' show Lena and Julia in their respective homes and Vanja in the studio trying out new songs, in all likelihood to be sung by someone else. Amongst them is a song called *Lyudi Invalidy* which will become the title track of the second t.A.T.u. album in a year's time. Meanwhile, Lena's dream of living in her own house in the centre of Moscow finally comes true, owing to all the free time she's enjoying since activity has been suspended.

On February 14, in the midst of the debacle, t.A.T.u. are invited to Singapore for the MTV Asia Awards. The girls and the director of Neformat, Bobza, are not sure what to do: it's a long way to go just to collect the prize without performing. They try recording a video message, but MTV won't accept it. A few hours before their flight is due to depart Bobza decides it's best to go, but Julia will not contemplate spending six hours on a plane, staying a few hours in Singapore and then spending another six hours on the return flight just to attend the ceremony, so she refuses. Lena, who was hoping to spend Valentine's Day in Moscow, reluctantly goes ahead without Julia and accepts the award for Favourite Breakthrough Act on behalf of t.A.T.u. alone. After the show, Lena uses the Podnebesnaya TV cameras in her hotel room to wish everybody she holds dear a happy Valentine's Day, but incredibly she doesn't mention Julia; only when this is pointed out to her does she add a simple 'hi' for the person who up until a few months ago was considered - albeit now revealed as a hoax - to be her life partner.

In the midst of this precarious period for t.A.T.u.'s artistic existence comes a proposal from the famous German rock group Rammstein to collaborate on a song[110]. What they have in mind is to ask the two famous Russian popstars to sing the chorus (in Russian) on their new song *Moskau*, which is dedicated to their hometown. It is not unlikely that Rammstein were thinking of t.A.T.u. when they first wrote the song, because the style and melody of the chorus seem perfectly adapted to the voices of Lena and Julia. Unfortunately - and also because of the decidedly inopportune timing – the managers of the two groups fail to reach an agreement: Lena remembers[111] that they were called back when they were actually on their way to the airport to go and record the song because their respective producers couldn't agree on which of the two groups should appear first in the credits. Rammstein eventually ask Victoria Fersch to do it, whose voice is so close to t.A.T.u.'s that many people still think it's Julia and Lena singing.

Meanwhile, episodes of the reality show continue to go out and Katya Nechaeva makes another appearance - the backing singer

---

[110] *"ТАТУ" споют с "Rammstein"*, Dni.ru, 4 April 2004.
[111] Караван историй, December 2011.

who was tipped to become a member of t.A.T.u. a year ago. Katya recalls that the management had even asked her to change her hairstyle in case she should be needed to join the group (to replace Volkova in all likelihood, because of her health problems). Remembering Nechaeva, Julia notes that at the time (2003) the backing singer seemed to be trying to copy everything she did, but in Lena's opinion nobody would ever dare to seriously consider replacing Julia:

> In other groups you can imagine replacing one of the members without too many adverse consequences, but for t.A.T.u. with their history and their image, it would be impossible to replace Julia or me with another singer. (Lena Katina, 2013)

Julia's 19th birthday comes round; February 20. The day before, Vanya had given her a present with an enigmatic message: 'something you can't do without' and when she opens it later at home it's a photo of Shapovalov. The message is clear, and when she discusses it with her father Julia has to admit that deep down she owes everything to Vanja, who has become very close to her over the last four years; but she also knows that much of the group's success is down to Elena Kiper and Sergio Galoyan. The same evening Julia is a guest on a TV show where she celebrates her birthday with her friends from SMASH! In a brief interview Volkova denies rumours of a move to a solo career: 'Lena and I are a duo, we stick together.'

When the reality show closes (Vanya finds out about it when the management of the Hotel Peking ask him to vacate the tower rooms by 1st March) and montages of video clips from concerts in 2003 are aired instead, Shapovalov suddenly unveils a new project at a press conference which is actually entitled 'Podnebesnaya: a collection of material recorded during the reality show with other artists who were guests in various episodes'. For the first time in five years, the creator of the t.A.T.u. project does not appear with the girls, does not mention them, and describes new ventures that do not seem to involve them.

The newspapers are quick to write t.A.T.u. off: Maksim Kononenko writes in the Gazeta[112] under the headline 'The Birth and Death of t.A.T.u.':

Julia and Lena have made a big mistake in voluntarily giving up the most powerful brand in Russia... As just singers they're nothing, there are plenty of other nineteen-year-olds in this country who can sing.

The journalist assumes that the t.A.T.u. brand remains the property of Shapovalov's Neformat, and that he intends to publish his album by various artists under this name.

And Shapovalov does indeed come close to it. The t.A.T.u. logo appears (very small) on the cover of the album *Podnebesnaya No.1*, using the same typeface as on Julia and Lena's first album. Among the thirteen songs on the CD is *Belochka,* with t.A.T.u. credited as the artists on the CD cover, but in fact it is sung just by Katina:

I had recorded the demo for *Belochka* some time earlier at the Neformat offices, one day when I was really ill and had a fever. It was supposed to be a t.A.T.u. song but Ivan liked it so much the way I sang it that he decided to keep it as a song just for my voice. Then he used the demo for the track on his album *Podnebesnaya.*(Lena Katina, 2013)

---

[112] Maksim Kononenko, *"Смерть и жизнь группы ТАТУ",* Gazeta, 2 March 2004.

T.A.T.U. ACT II

In late March of 2004, 'battleship Tary', which had conquered the world just a year ago, is now drifting out to sea at the mercy of the currents. The main driving force that kept them on the crest of the wave for four years - their image as two scandalous teenage lesbians - has now been permanently switched off; the captain of the ship, Shapovalov, has been deposed by Julia and Lena's mutiny, and now there's nobody at the helm. Even the cannons have run out of ammunition: t.A.T.u. have no new songs (*Nich'ya* can't be a single) and the last thing they released – not counting remixes and concert DVDs - is the 2003 Eurovision song. What's more, in the last twelve months they've neglected their fans and done only four concerts because of Julia's ongoing voice problems (Bonn in June, two in Tokyo in December and their last one in St. Petersburg, also in December).

Under these conditions it's hard to prevent the ship sailing into oblivion: youngsters soon grow up, forget their idols and replace them with new, trendier ones. The critics know this and they begin to commemorate the passing of the group, some of them with undisguised satisfaction such as Paul Hounds and Will Stewart in their article[113] in the Daily Mail, evocatively titled 'The curse of Tatu', in which they reconstruct the story of Julia and Lena, their pact with the devil and their meagre financial returns compared to the fortune that Shapovalov has amassed.

But not everyone has jumped ship so soon. Certainly not Elena Kiper, former PR and author of t.A.T.u.'s first two hits, who has

---

[113] Paul Stewart Will Hunting Hounds *"The curse of Tat,," Daily Mail*, 25 March 2004.

long been in open conflict with her ex-partner Shapovalov. Kiper, who is awaiting the verdict on her legal action against Neformat, publicly offers[114] her services to the group's new management, not directly as their songwriter but in terms of coordinating their image, the style of music and the lyrics etc.

The scene of the second act in the story of t.A.T.u. is now taking shape: Shapovalov will give up direction of Neformat (the company that owns the group's trademark) and the role of producer; Galoyan will return as songwriter for the group, and financers (Rensky in the first place) will accept Kiper's offer (who will not, however, give up her financial claims to the copyright of the English versions of *All The Things She Said* and *Not Gonna Get Us*). Kiper has a new image in mind for Lena and Julia which represents a complete break from the scandalistic Shapovalov era. The official role of producer which was occupied by Shapovalov will now be held by TA Music, recently set up by Rensky and - it seems - the girls, and a new deal with Universal International has already been negotiated. This will ensure aerial support for 'battleship Тату' in the turbulent international waters.

The jigsaw that was in disarray now seems to have all the pieces in place, but nothing is ever simple for t.A.T.u. In late April Julia officially announces that she is in her third month of pregnancy. Pasha Sidorov is the baby's father: the martial arts champion who has accompanied her everywhere for the past year and who has left his wife and daughter for her.

Because of the pregnancy the concert scheduled in the USA for May is cancelled and all other performances are put off until the end of September, after the baby is born. But Julia is determined to continue working in the studio on songs for the new album, at least up until August. The songs are immediately selected in London by Martin Kierszenbaum (also known under his show business

---

[114] *Елена Кипер предложила новому менеджменту группы "Тату" сотрудничество,* Artconsult.ru, 25 March 2004.

pseudonym of Cherry Cherry Boom Boom) of Interscope, in a meeting with Galoyan. Sergio has been living in England for some time and this circumstance will prove significant for the new direction that t.A.T.u.'s style takes from this point on. Galoyan remembers:

> At that time I was deeply influenced by a sound that was very popular in England: the rock band. When Martin came to London and I played him five or six of these rock demos, he said 'ok, those are fine, that's the way the market is going.' This was a big mistake for which I take full responsibility, because t.A.T.u. were not a rock band, they were more dance or dubstep. Our fans loved us for our dance rhythm and tunes, and this was the main reason for the decline in popularity of the group. (Sergio Galoyan, 2012)[115]

In keeping with their more adult and often melancholy style of music, the lyrics of the new t.A.T.u. songs reflect the new course of the supposed relationship between the girls: the story of adolescent love depicted in their early songs turns into a representation of conflict between them after Julia's 'betrayal' of Lena with the man who gave her a child. With song titles like *Loves Me Not, Friend or Foe* and *Perfect Enemy* fans will already have the impression that they are totally autobiographical before they even get to the lyrics; they have no idea that neither Julia nor Lena had anything to do with writing the words.

On June 7, the Moscow City Court issues a judgment in favour of Elena Kiper in the case brought against Neformat for non-payment of royalties on the English versions of *Ya Soshla S Uma* and *Nas Ne Dogonyat:* Kiper will receive royalties for all albums sold[116] and 500,000 rubles in compensation.

---

[115] Quote given by Sergio Galoyan in person to the author, 2012

[116] *Прорывом,* Artconsult.ru, 8 June 2004.

On the evening of July 9 Julia feels ill[117] and is rushed to the clinic fearing she may go into premature labour. When the crisis is over the doctors forbid her to work any more in the time remaining before delivery, at the end of September. The release date for the album, planned for the end of the year in an agreement with Universal that they signed in June, is now adjourned *sine die*.

In July and August Lena continues to work alone, recording demos with Galoyan in Moscow for a number of tracks chosen for the new album (*Cosmos, Sacrifice, Vsya Moya Lyubov*), and others that are never completed like *You* (aka *I Miss You*) also by Galoyan (who records it himself the following year). The press fills the void left by the partial inactivity of t.A.T.u. with news and gossip about Lena: first it's announced that she intends to follow a solo career parallel with being in the group[118], then a collaboration with singer Rina Rock (whose producer is her father Sergey Katin)[119] and finally her impending marriage with ex-boyfriend Andrey. The last two rumours (but not the solo project which Lena herself later confirms) are denied by Neformat's PR, Aleksandra Tityanko.

On September 23 Julia delivers little Vika (Viktoria) naturally, and the news is reported in the mainstream press. The Sun takes the opportunity[120] to announce the return of t.A.T.u. to Europe in November for a grand concert at Wembley organised by Trevor Horn to celebrate his 25 years in the business, with proceeds to the Prince's Trust. The British daily, which has never been sympathetic towards t.A.T.u., doesn't fail to express much concern about the group's future now that they've dumped their exciting outrageous image.

---

[117] *"ТАТУШКА" Юли проблемы со здоровьем*, Dni.ru, 12 July 2004.
[118] *Лена Катина займется сольной карьерой*, Dni.ru, 20 May 2004.
[119] *"Лене Катиной нашли новую ТАТУШКУ"*, Komsomolskaya Pravda, 30 July 2004.
[120] *"Tatu faced"*, The Sun, 21 September 2004.

On the first of October Komsomolskaya Pravda[121] publishes a long interview with Lena Katina, in which she confirms, amongst other things, her plans for a solo album to be produced by her father. Asked about her current relationship with Volkova, Lena admits that she didn't go to the clinic to see her after the birth, but only because Julia expressly asked her not to.

> We're not friends, we're sisters. We've been through so much together that we're like family now. Of course, we have different views on certain things, but it's not a problem. The main thing is that we can't do without each other. (Lena Katina, 2004)

On 16th October Lena and Julia (in public for the first time after the birth of her child) take part in the MTV Russian Music Awards as guests of honour to present their friends in SMASH! with the award for Best Russian Group of the year. Julia seems to be on reasonable form and is carrying only a little extra weight after her pregnancy, while Lena with straightened hair and eye-catching make-up is finally looking all of her beautiful twenty years.

But t.A.T.u.'s first real performance in their new incarnation comes at the Trevor Horn concert at Wembley where Julia appears with newly ash-blond hair, and Lena with her natural curly hair trimmed unusually short; both are dressed in plain white tee-shirts and denim shorts. Lip-synching to *All The Things She Said* the girls embrace each other and hold hands on stage, but like two sisters now: nothing that could give rise to any malicious interpretation. The new image leaves the younger members of the audience a little confused: news of the abrupt change of course for 'battleship Тату' has obviously not been widespread in Europe like it was at home, and those who expected t.A.T.u.to come out as wild, rebellious and provocative as in 2003 are bitterly disappointed.

---

[121] *"ТАТУШКА" Лена Катина: Брошу курить и тоже рожу девочку!* "Komsomolskaya Pravda, 1 October 2004.

That they have distanced themselves from the schoolgirls-in-love image of the Shapovalov era is quite clear.

The use of lip-synching at Wembley was a device intended not only to reflect the importance of the event, but according to the Express Gazeta[122] was necessitated by Julia's recurring voice problems, probably brought on by a postnatal hormone imbalance, and as a result recording of the new album is once again suspended. Unofficial biographies often identify this latest withdrawal of Julia's as the period in which she underwent an alleged operation on her vocal chords, but this rumour has never been officially confirmed.

By mid-December, however, the condition of Julia's voice seems improved: t.A.T.u. take part in a charity concert organised in Moscow for relatives of victims of the Beslan massacre (a terrorist attack at a school in September where 334 people were killed, including 186 children). Julia and Lena perform *Nich'ya*, *How Soon Is Now* and *Show Me Love*, singing mostly live.

2004, the traumatic year that marked their turning point, ends on a downturn for t.A.T.u: they are awarded the title of 'worst band' by the lesbian magazine AfterEllen[123] (which only the year before was defending their image to the hilt[124]) on the grounds of 'having affected a lesbian relationship for mere profit, letting many lesbian and bisexual teenagers down and making a mockery of themselves and of female homosexuality.'

---

[122] Nikita Belov *"У ТАТУШКИ СНОВА пропал голос"*, Express Gazeta, 26 November 2004.
[123] Sarah Warn *The 1st Annual AfterEllen.com Visibility Awards* Afterellen.com, 22 December 2004.
[124] Rob and Nike Breezay *In Defense of tATu*, Afterellen.com, October 2003.

DANGEROUS & MOVING

2005 starts with a wedding within the staff group: t.A.T.u.'s current PR Aleksandra Tityanko marries musician Sergio (Sergey) Galoyan, who wrote the group's early successes and is now working on the new album, and who also occupies the new role of sound producer. Lena and Julia, of course, attend the ceremony which is held a few days before their departure to Los Angeles where they will be staying for a few weeks whilst they finish recordings at the prestigious Village Studios where many famous recording artists have worked, from the Beatles to Madonna.

Julia's voice problems are still a major obstacle to the success of the work and Interscope decide to seek the advice of one of the greatest vocal coaches in the world, Ron Anderson, who has worked with the likes of Kylie Minogue and Bjork in the past to eliminate voice-related problems. Julia is subjected to long daily exercises over several weeks to get used to the method that Anderson recommends to enable her to produce the 'screeching' effect without straining her already delicate vocal chords.

As a result recording sessions proceed very slowly, and they also have two separate albums to complete; one in English (which is given priority) and another version in Russian. In April, the Russian press[125] takes up a story reported in Zhizn, according to which Lena and Julia are about to return to Moscow to settle an argument between them as to who should be the main voice on one of the songs being recorded, to be mediated by Neformat staff. Julia and Lena do return to Moscow, but only because Lena has to

---

[125] *Запись нового альбома "ТАТУ" сорвалась*, Newsmusic.ru, 26 April 2005.

have a gallbladder operation after experiencing serious stomach pains in Los Angeles. A year afterwards Lena confesses in a television broadcast[126] that she feared for her life over this.

Julia takes part in celebrations for the launch of a new fashion magazine in late April, and during an interview with MTV Russia on the occasion, confirms that the English version of the album is almost finished and that she's going straight back to Los Angeles to start recording the Russian version. Lena joins her on May 12 after a short convalescence.

On 3rd June t.A.T.u. are invited to the Muz TV National Awards as guests of honour. The girls arrive at the Olympiysky Arena in Moscow well ahead of time to attend the pre-show VIP party, where they have to rely on being recognised by the doormen to get in, as the organisers have not provided them with passes.

In the months leading up to the event Muz TV has been billing the return of t.A.T.u. as the main attraction, and the large hall is buzzing with anticipation for their performance, expecting it to cause an outrage more than a sensation.

The lights go on after starting in total darkness, to reveal Julia and Lena standing on top of a high tower dressed in very short black shift dresses with bare legs and feet (Lena says in her online journal that Julia bought the dresses and had them shortened by a tailor). They keep the same position, holding hands and not singing, whilst a remixed instrumental version of *Ya Soshla S Uma* plays out, to the delight of the crowd who are amazed not to hear them singing.

The idea was clearly to iconify the return of the two global teen stars, now grown up and sexy: the monolith, the darkness followed by dramatic uplighting, flames coming from an enormous structure to the side, and the tune of their greatest hit without the words. Julia and Lena only manage to remain in character for less than a minute though, then they smile, say something to each other, and

---

[126] *"100 вопросов к взрослому"*, TVC, 30 September 2006.

Lena even chuckles. It occurs to Julia to gesture the audience to sing, but the instrumental version of the song has a different arrangement and the original lyrics don't fit, so - quite rightly - the crowd don't take her up on it. What should have been a memorable moment becomes almost a pantomime.

Things go a little better after another interval of darkness: Julia and Lena walk down two flights of metal steps (somewhat unsteadily) to the opening notes of *Obezyanka Nol'*, a new song that will be included in the new album they're working on, which fortunately they perform in the traditional way on stage.

The next day Russian critics are not kind to t.A.T.u.: online music magazine Zvuki.ru calls[127] the show 'a perfect demonstration of the end of the project,' and Komsomolskaya Pravda, referring to the skimpy outfits worn by Lena and Julia, headlines with[128] 'Not even stripping can save Tatu' and doesn't omit to point out that their figures are a little fuller than before.

At the same time news of the new album is starting to spread: the title of the Russian version will be *Lyudi Invalidy* (Disabled People), while the English version will be *Dangerous & Moving*. The friendly participation of Sting is announced, who will play his legendary Fender P-Bass in the song *Friend Or Foe* which also boasts Dave Stewart of Eurythmics as one of the writers, and the collaboration of Richard Carpenter of The Carpenters in *Gomenasai*, all thanks to the intervention of the illustrious Martin Kierszenbaum as co-writer and producer of six of the twelve songs on the album. Lena and Julia don't actually get to meet Sting (who records his part in New York) or the other famous people who collaborate, with the exception of Trevor Horn who plays an active part in the recording and production process, and Carpenter, but

---

[127] Alexander Gorbachev *"Премия" Муз-ТВ"*, Zvuki.ru, 6 June 2005.

[128] Maria Elena Remizova Lapteva *"Поп-певиц не надо слушать - на них надо смотреть"*, *Komsomolskaya Pravda*, 5 June 2005.

only several months later whilst they're filming the video for *Friend or Foe*.

Lena is back in Los Angeles the day after the TV show, whilst Julia stays on in Moscow a few days longer. The tabloid press put Julia's delay down to the sudden breakup of her relationship with Pasha Sidorov[129]; a few days later Julia herself confirms her separation from Vika's father in her online journal.

The pace of work in Los Angeles starts to pick up towards the end of the month; between stints of recording songs in Russian Julia and Lena are also involved in photo shoots for covers, posters and promotional material for the two albums. The girls also meet up with their official band again after a gap of many months, to try out the new songs live and get used to working with them again, and for the first time they meet their new manager who will be opening up the US market for them. This is the well-known Caresse Henry who was managing Madonna up until a year ago. Unfortunately though, in true t.A.T.u. style, this opportunity is also irretrievably lost within a few weeks. Lena recounts:

> At Interscope they were adamant that we had to have a manager at all costs, and we were considering various possibilities, such as Michael Brokaw and then Caresse Henry, with whom we began to build up a relationship around the time we were having the controversy with Interscope over the song Gomenasai. Boris felt that the manager should always support the artist, but not when the artist is wrong, as was the case here [*author's note:* the girls and Boris did not want to include Gomenasai on the album because they didn't think it matched their style]. That's why I think Boris was wrong in wanting to break off the relationship with Caresse. (Lena Katina, 2013)

---

[129] Oleg Goncharov "" *ТАТУШКА "ЮЛЯ выгнала мужа,"* *Express Gazeta*, 24 June 2005.

Lena returns to Moscow for a few days at the beginning of July after completing her recording sessions, whilst Julia, who is a little behind, stays in Los Angeles. They meet up again on July 18, the day before filming starts for the *All About Us* and *Lyudi Invalidy* videos.

Documentary-style videos - as we have seen - have always been central to t.A.T.u.'s winning formula from the start, and for the two new videos Universal and the group's managers decide to hire innovative Hollywood director James Cox.

All About Us is planned as the first single release from the album, and is therefore the track that will drive it; for the video Cox manages to link up t.A.T.u.'s old hackneyed lesbian image with their new less sexually-explicit adult image to create a video that will appeal to both old and new fans. Since sexual outrage is no longer a viable theme (even though the substance of the relationship between the two girls was largely left to the imagination of observers to determine) the shock factor now turns to violence: the images of Julia being subjected to beatings and her aggressor having his head blown off at close range are reminiscent of Quentin Tarantino's Pulp style of ten years ago, but have not been used before in a music video, and especially not one where the artists are two pretty nineteen-year-old pop singers and not a heavy metal band. High-minded Americans will also be disturbed that the video is a bad example for youngsters on a number of counts: from Julia's casual alcohol drinking as she walks the streets at night scantily dressed, then taking up with a stranger, to Lena's dangerous driving: she steers a powerful Chevrolet Camaro 396 one-handed and without a seatbelt whilst talking into a mobile phone. Not to mention the use of firearms.

To avoid the same problems of censorship and boycott that plagued the video for *All The Things She Said,* a softer version is also prepared for television, cutting the scene where Julia gives the finger (replaced by a closed fist), the beatings and the whole shooting scene (these two scenes are replaced with images of Julia alone in the room). The censored version, which is released first, loses much of its impact and appeal.

Cox also records the video for *Lyudi Invalidy* at the same time, using practically the same set (the street in the final scene of the first video is the same one in the second video). This video is also intended to cause a sensation, showing Lena and Julia plunged into a society which is depraved in the extreme, albeit as bewildered observers. Shooting of the video is marred by sanitary problems; it is shot in one of the worst suburbs of Los Angeles and many of the extras are actual vagrants recruited from the neighbourhood streets. Some of the characters in the video suffer from a variety of disabilities, and Cox's decision to use them complicates the task that t.A.T.u. already have in explaining that the song lyrics mean 'disabled' in the sense of men without heart and conscience and therefore 'unable' to have feelings and love for others. This explanation is also clearly supported in Russian in the booklet inserted with the CD which, translated, means, 'their actions are driven by the laws of mechanics and four other ideals: cruelty, stupidity, greed, depravity,' but this is not enough to sanction the video or the track which is never released as a single for this very reason, even though it's the preferred choice of Julia and Lena as the second single after *All About Us*.

In late July Lena and Julia finally return to Moscow for a rest after nearly seven months in Los Angeles, before starting the promotional tour for the new album. Meanwhile, the press reveal more unconfirmed reports about the long-awaited return of t.A.T.u. The Japanese newspaper Sankei Sports[130] reports that the song *Gomenasai* (from the Japanese *'gomen nasai'*, 'I'm sorry') is dedicated to Japanese fans as an apology for what happened in 2003 when t.A.T.u. suddenly walked out of a TV show without performing, and the British press are focussing attention on the

---

[130] *"謝罪ソング「ゴメナサイ!"* Sankei Sports, 2 August 2005.

scandalistic content of the video for *All About Us:* 'Julia and Lena have turned their dubious talents towards bloody murder and domestic violence,' writes the News Of The World[131] with their usual British skepticism towards the group.

The single *All About Us* is released to radio stations at the beginning of August and official distribution begins in Japan as announced on 1st September. The video (censored version) is made available on the internet on August 18 and its first TV showing is by the ITV channel in Britain on the 21st, on the music programme CD UK .

All About Us (which features amongst its writers Julia & Lena's contemporaries, the Italo-Australian Origliasso twins, known as The Veronicas) gets a lukewarm reception in Japan contrary to expectation and is relegated to the bottom of the charts.

Lyudi Invalidy has its debut on Russian radio stations at the beginning of September.

In the meantime Julia and Lena commence promotion of the new album in Europe. On 31st August they are guests on 'Punkt12' on the RTL Germany TV channel, then fly to Barcelona, where the whole band is waiting to accompany them for the whole promo-tour in France, Italy, Germany, Britain, Finland and Sweden. The programme for the performances - as Sven Martin recalls - will initially consist of just four or five songs, and this will gradually be expanded over successive months, culminating in the final programme the following year.

Lena and Julia are dressed as in the *All About Us* video in TV and stage appearances, which means that Julia often has to wear a black wig in a bob style as her natural hair has been cropped very short. In the dozens of interviews they do Lena and Julia explain that the lyrics for *All About Us* are inspired by their own lives and that the hazard symbols on *Dangerous & Moving* (the yellow and black stripes on the cover graphics) normally appear as a danger

---

[131] *"Tatu bad for telly"*, News of the World, 21 August 2005.

warning on machinery, but in life the greatest danger comes from humans with no conscience and no feelings *(Lyudi Invalidy)*.

In the two days they spend in Italy (15 and 16 September), Lena and Julia meet their fans at Caffè Fiat in Milan, where a lucky group of about thirty fans receive copies of a promo CD containing remixed versions of *All About Us* autographed by the girls, who also have their pictures taken with their fans. After this t.A.T.u. make a recording of *All About Us* for the Top Of The Pops programme for RAI at Mediaset.

A live performance of *All About Us* is scheduled for September 17 on the CD UK programme. Lena and Julia ask if they can come on carrying two real pistols (as they did in Monte Carlo in 2003) in keeping with the video image, but the director of the ITV show categorically refuses and the girls just turn up dressed as in the video. In the evening Julia and Lena perform at the G.A.Y. Club (their first real gig with the band, as Sven Martin recalls) and a few days later they return to Moscow for little Vika's first birthday party.

On 28th September, in the middle of the promotional tour, Julia and Lena announce in an awkward TV interview on the German music show VIVA that they have split with Caresse Henry due to a clash of personalities, but without giving any other details,

On 3rd October, a week after official distribution is launched in the rest of the world (it was released in Japan on 1st September) the single *All About Us* debuts on the European charts, including Britain, and reaches number eight. Two days earlier t.A.T.u. performed live at Glam As You Party in Paris.

After celebrating her twentieth birthday in Moscow Lena joins Julia in Japan for a promotional mini-tour during which they give interviews, meet fans and record an interview and a performance for the popular 'Utaban Show.' The programme is recorded to avoid the same problems as in 2003: the presenter (singer

Masahiro Nakai of SMAP) makes explicit reference to this, saying ironically[132] 'please don't walk out in the middle of the show.'

On October 13, instead of the scheduled trip to Israel as part of the promotion, t.A.T.u. fly to Los Angeles to shoot the video for *Friend Or Foe*, with the same director: Cox. Universal has brought forward the date for filming because they intend to release the track as the second single from the album instead of *Dangerous & Moving* which it was initially going to be. The video is shot over 16th and 17th October inside the Bronson Caves in the Hollywood Hills, which was used as the set for the Batman TV series in the 1960s. The plot is very simple: Lena and Julia drive into a cavern at full speed in a 1972 Chevrolet Chevelle SS convertible where they meet up with their (real) band and some friends to rehearse before a concert. Whilst they're rehearsing they get so into the song that the cavern soon turns into an impromptu disco. Richard Carpenter is also on the set.

On October 18 Julia and Lena return to Moscow for the official launch of the *Lyudi Invalidy* album (*Dangerous & Moving* was launched in the rest of the world a few days before) scheduled for 21st October in the Soyuz MediaHyperMarket, where the girls meet fans, sign autographs and do a live performance.

A week later t.A.T.u. perform in the Russian capital again, at the Gaudi Arena. Despite being late as usual, Julia and Lena and their live band manage to electrify the audience of fans and VIPs, singing eight songs from their new album live.

> Between the end of 2005 and the beginning of 2006 we gradually expanded the programme of our live performances from five or six songs at the G.A.Y. Club in London to 45 minutes on stage at Gaudi Arena in Moscow. (Sven Martin, 2012)

---

[132] *"Utaban Show"*, *TBS*, 27 October 2005.

Meanwhile, whilst *All About Us* is starting to climb the singles charts in Europe, the first reviews of the new album appear in the specialist press, and as usual they're mixed. Barry Walters of Rollingstone[133] does not deny the 'pleasure of the dark-dance-pop hits' but at the same time challenges the too simple melodies of some of the songs and eventually concludes that 'this t.A.T.u. wasn't designed to last'. Musicologist Stephen Thomas Erlewine of Allmusic[134] agrees, saying that 'without the sapphic gimmick, t.A.T.u. simply doesn't have a reason to exist.'

Roger Holland of PopMatters[135] is of the completely opposite opinion; he compares t.A.T.u. to ABBA and Madonna, and pointing out that the girls are at their best singing in their own language, concludes with dispassionate praise for *Obezyanka Nol'* in which 'Emotion offered by Lena and Yulya's quite distinct vocal ranges touches places most pop music couldn't find with a map and GPS.'

Such conflicting judgments from the experts would be incomprehensible but for the explanation provided by t.A.T.u.'s beginnings: a music venture set up by virtual amateurs in a country that had never had a band achieve worldwide acclaim before, and launched in an entirely new (and probably dubious) way. But more importantly, a phenomenon that managed to exist outside the accepted, though unwritten, rules of show business in the western world, at least for the time that Shapovalov was the manager and for some time after that too, and seems destined to carry on paying the price for such a radical decision.

On 3rd November Julia and Lena are invited to take part in the MTV Europe Music Awards as guests, to present Robbie Williams with the ward for Best Singer of the Year. Accepting the trophy, Williams - clearly out of touch with the girls' recently altered

---

[133] Barry Walters' *Dangerous and Moving reviews, Rolling Stone,* 19 October 2005.
[134] Stephen Thomas Erlewine *Dangerous and Moving reviews,* Allmusic.com
[135] Roger Holland *t.A.T.u: Dangerous and Moving,* Popmatters.com, 7 October 2005.

situation - turns to Julia and Lena and says 'I love your love for women.'

A week later t.A.T.u. resume their promotional tour; first stop Copenhagen, where Julia and Lena take part in a few TV shows and meet the local press, then Paris, London (where they perform at Glam As You), and finally back to Paris. The promo-tour is fast-paced and not everything goes right, as noted by Sven:

> We had to fly from London to Paris with a little-known airline. We'd already boarded and from the window I saw all our equipment being loaded on the plane but my keyboards were still on the trolley and the driver was reading a newspaper and drinking coffee. I started to get worried because I knew that we'd be taking off in 10 minutes so I called the flight attendant who told me not to worry and that all our baggage would be loaded. Shortly after I heard the engines start, the lights went off and the plane started to move: I rang the bell frantically to call the steward back, who at that point admitted that nothing more could be done. My keyboards were left irretrievably behind. (Sven Martin, 2012)

t.A.T.u. finally arrive in Italy on 25th November. In Milan, Julia and Lena first meet journalists at the Italian headquarters of Universal, then go to MTV's attic studio in Cathedral Square to appear live on Total Request Live. t.A.T.u. are treated with greater respect by the Italian presenters this time than they were three years ago, and the interview passes much more smoothly thanks to Julia's improved grasp of English from spending all those months in Los Angeles. The crowds waiting in Cathedral Square for Julia and Lena to wave from the balcony, however, are only half what they were in 2002. A little later t.A.T.u. go down to the nearby Messaggerie Musicali to sign autographs and CDs, and in the evening they fly to Rome. In the capital, Julia and Lena take part in the live afternoon show 'Amici' di Maria De Filippi, where they sing *All About Us* accompanied by the band, give radio interviews, meet fans, but their live performance scheduled for Sunday on the RAI 1 TV channel's 'Domenica In' is cancelled.

The same evening t.A.T.u. leave for South America to continue their promotional tour. The first stop is Mexico where they receive an enthusiastic welcome: ever since their first international launch South America has always held an enormous reserve of fans devoted to Julia and Lena. The girls repay their affection with an extended live performance at Club Salon 21 (vastly overcrowded), broadcast live by the most popular music TV channel in Latin America, Telehit. t.A.T.u. have included *Obezyanka Nol '* in the programme: the most exciting song on the new album but also one that puts an enormous strain on Julia's fragile voice. Julia feels her vocal chords straining almost immediately, but stoically and generously carries on singing to the end of the song whilst Lena gives her frequent opportunities to rest by offering the microphone to the crowd so that they can sing in her place. At the end of the show, after *All The Things She Said,* the audience loudly urge Julia and Lena to kiss, but the girls restrict themselves to blowing a kiss to the cheering crowd.

On 1st December they're in Argentina, where they give interviews and perform on two different TV programmes in as many days, in Buenos Aires.

The South American tour concludes in Brazil where, amongst other bookings, Julia and Lena are guests of the most watched television talk show, the Jo Soares Show. The girls are well-loved in Sao Paolo too, and the Urban Club where they perform their mini concert is packed and airless. This, together with the excessive heat and high levels of amplification, leave Julia and Lena so exhausted by the end of the set as to require medical attention; it's nothing serious, but they are left totally exhausted and have to cancel their appearance on a live MTV Brazil show.

The next day t.A.T.u. fly to the other side of the globe, to Taiwan. It's their first time in Taipei, and after arriving a day late due to a hold-up in Frankfurt over visa complications, Julia and Lena appear at a crowded press conference attended by journalists from several Asian countries. Once again the press demonstrate that they are ill-informed about t.A.T.u.'s recent revelations and Julia is asked yet again to clarify the nature of her relationship with Lena. Julia gives the same reply that she's been repeating for the last year: 'there's deep feeling between us - we've known each other for over 10 years - but we've never claimed to be lesbians. We love each other, we're like sisters, there's nothing immoral in it.' It's all up in the air again soon after though, when she talks about how she and Lena spent the night before apart, saying, 'I can't sleep without her,' which gives the presenter an open invitation to reply ironically, 'be careful when you sleep together.' The next evening, t.A.T.u. perform live with the whole band at the Chun-Shen stadium in front of almost 40,000 spectators - mainly youngsters - which is broadcast live on television.

Taipei is the last stage of the promotional tour that takes place in 2005. Before the end of the year Julia and Lena also perform in Zurich as part of the big charity concert 'Energy Stars For Free' along with other pop stars. During this time the official website announces that Guy Chambers, a well-known songwriter and co-producer of many of Robbie Williams' albums, has written a song for t.A.T.u. called *Wrapped Around Your Fingers* that the group will just include in their live shows for the moment. The news arouses quite some interest because of Chambers' high profile, but the agreement with Chambers is never finalised[136] and the song is never included in t.A.T.u.'s repertoire.

---

[136] Tatu.ru official blog, *Insider* post, 27 August 2007.

DANGEROUS & MOVING TOUR

2006 is the golden year for t.A.T.u. in terms of live performances. Finally, after all the problems associated with Julia's voice in 2003, the split with Shapovalov, Julia's pregnancy in 2004 and the long period spent in the US to record the album in 2005, the girls are now back, and able to devote all their time to doing live performances and concerts.

Their first official event of the year is in Helsinki, where the NJR Radio Awards are being held on January 19; one of the biggest music accolades in Scandinavia. Julia and Lena are nominated for Best Pop Group and Best International Group and they win both awards; during the show they perform *All About Us*.

Two days later the girls are in Budapest where they are guests of honour at the Hungarian Grammies and perform *All About Us* (lip-synching) and *Friend or Foe* (singing live) - the second single from the album currently being distributed in Europe - and close with *All The Things She Said*.

On January 25 Lena and Julia are back to London to make some television appearances and perform at the G.A.Y. club again.

In February, the single *Friend Or Foe* is starting to climb the charts in Europe when Interscope announce that the third single from the album *Dangerous & Moving* will be *Gomenasai*. The song, written by Martin Kierszenbaum, was not originally planned as a single - as we know: Julia and Lena didn't even want to record it - so making a video to go with it was never thought of, but Interscope (of which Kierszenbaum is an executive) unexpectedly decides to give it precedence over *Dangerous & Moving*.

> Gomenasai was a good idea: it was a nice, simple song, but t.A.T.u. songs were neither nice nor simple - they were controversial and complex. We knew that Gomenasai wasn't in keeping with our image and that's why we tried to reject the song, but Interscope was against us. (Lena Katina, 2013)

In the first few days of the new year an interesting rapping-style cover of Gomenasai had been released under the title *Happy Birthday* by a band called Flipsyde - a band signed to the same record label as t.A.T.u. In it, the band reads a sort of letter to an unborn aborted child, and use two lines from the original song by Lena and Julia, so the artists are credited as Flipsyde feat. t.A.T.u. and the girls, although they don't appear in the video for it, do actively participate in promoting the single on television in 2006. The cover by Flipsyde reaches higher chart positions than *Gomenasai*.

After a relaxing February in Moscow where Julia celebrates her twenty-first birthday with her family, t.A.T.u. resume their promo-tour in March, starting in Germany where they promote *Happy Birthday* along with Flipsyde on the TV shows TRL and Top of the Pops.

Julia and Lena then return to Los Angeles where they record the video for *Gomenasai* and meet new arrivals in the band, drummer Steve Wilson (replacing Roman Raetej) and bassist Domen Vajevec (a bassist was needed for the sound of their new songs). This time Hype Williams is chosen as the director: a video specialist who uses the metropolitan botanical gardens in California as the location. Williams alternates images of the stone angels and fountains in the park with soft-focus close-ups of Lena and Julia on a black background. In the video, the shot with Julia in profile in the foreground and Lena in the background, with focus alternating between the two, is so similar to Agnetha and Frida in

ABBA's video for *Fernando* in 1976 that they should be actually listed in the credits for it. The video, as well as the actual song, is quite a departure from t.A.T.u.'s usual style and leaves many of their fans cold.

There is also a second, fully animated, version of the video which is released before the official one and broadcast by a few music TV stations. In the manga-style animated video set in the future, Julia is a heroine called to save Lena from the clutches of an evil scientist who holds her captive.

On 18th March t.A.T.u.. are in Hamburg, Germany with the band in its new formation, where they perform as part of the NRJ Music Tour. Six days later Julia and Lena are scheduled to perform a preview of their set for the upcoming *Dangerous & Moving* tour at the Rush Hour club in Dortmund. Lena has the flu and skips a lot of the rehearsals so Julia has to sing both parts in rehearsals with the band, but Lena manages to recover in time for the show.

A week later Julia and Lena return to Milan for the Italian TRL Awards ceremony where they win the award for Best Group. They perform *All About Us* and *Gomenasai* in lip-sync.

t.A.T.u. are expected in Santiago, Chile, on 1st April for what should be the opening concert of the *Dangerous & Moving* promo tour, but before the girls leave Italy the visit to the South American country is postponed by twenty days because of alleged problems with entry visas. The local press[137], however, report that with less than a week to go before the event only 3,000 of the 9,000 tickets available have been sold. Two weeks later a further attempt at postponement fails when one of the sponsors withdraws and the event is cancelled altogether.

The debut tour date then becomes 11th April in a place where they have more amicable relations: Tallinn in Estonia. But actually the Suurhall Saku Arena, which has a capacity of 10,000, is only half full and the audience remains unimpressed when they see Lena and

---

[137] Carola Reyes, *Postergan concierto en Chile* Terra.cl, 17 April 2006.

Julia appear on stage wearing fur coats: untypical for them. The atmosphere warms when the girls change on stage into their customary style, and later when they sing their early hits. Apart from a few sound problems the concert goes ahead as planned without any major setbacks and at the end they do an encore of *All About Us*.

The next day the girls are in Riga, Latvia. The programme is the same, and again the Kipsala Hall is only half full. The papers report[138] a partial flop: Julia's voice problems aside (this is their second full concert in 24 hours), t.A.T.u.'s early fans will clearly have to get used to the group's new low-key rock style.

> Technically, the live performances could have been better if we'd spent a little more time rehearsing, but it was always difficult to detain the girls for very long. (Sven Martin, 2012)

At the same time the Russian music channel MUZ TV commences broadcasts of a new programme entitled 't.A.T.u. Expedition,' similar to a reality show, portraying the lives of Julia and Lena over the thirty day period from mid-March to mid-April 2006. In 'Expedition' Lena and Julia seem much more mature and independent than in the past: a statement by Neil Jacobson of Interscope confirms:

> They're very determined. They always seem to know the right thing to do, they know when they're right and when they're wrong. And I'm always trying to talk them into doing something and I'll try to get them to do something they may not want to do. While other artists will just do it, they trust me. But with the girls we spend 20 or 30 minutes arguing until they will agree to do something or not. Sometimes it's extremely frustrating, but it's

---

[138] Yulia Fomchenko *Концерт "ТАТУШЕК" в Риге провалился*, TVNET, 13 April 2006.

very rewarding because in the end they are usually right. (Neil Jacobson, 2006)

The reality show consists of 18 episodes and reveals the frenetic pace that Julia and Lena work at: travelling, interviews, rehearsals, concerts, meetings with fans etc. The members of the band also appear in the programme; they've become an integral part of the group by now, since the girls almost always sing live for their tour concerts. The public also get to see Julia and Lena's most private moments such as meetings with childhood friends, and even go into their hotel room: the girls have never concealed the fact that they share a bed when they're away from home and take the opportunity to tell how in their sleep, in contrast with their waking hours, Julia is the quieter one whilst Lena tosses and turns all night.

The third leg of the *Dangerous & Moving* promo tour is in St. Petersburg. Julia and Lena arrive behind schedule and their part in the TV show 'Family Matters' on Channel 5 is recorded late in the evening. Julia arrives at the studio wearing a provocative t-shirt that says 'fuck me I'm famous' and the atmosphere soon becomes heated, with Lena protesting that the on-cue applause demanded of the audience is over the top, and Julia quarrelling with the presenter when he asks the now pointless question about their emotional relationship. As a result the show ends with questions from the public (the presenter puts an end to the interview) and lasts much less than the 45 minutes planned.

The concert on April 28 is due to start at 7 o'clock in the evening, but as usual Julia and Lena are late and the band only starts playing the first notes of the introduction to *Lyudi Invalidy* well after 8. St. Petersburg has always been t.A.T.u.'s favourite place because the audience are so enthusiastic, and the girls are not disappointed. Julia and Lena put everything into what is the most important concert of the first part of the tour and will be recorded by the

MUZ TV cameras for release on DVD under the title Truth: Live in St. Petersburg. The DVD however is beset with problems in true t.A.T.u. style, and is only released in 2007.

Although the Peterburgsky Arena is not completely sold out and there are plenty of empty seats, the concert is hailed in the press as a great success in terms of the performance: Artur Gasparyan in Moskovskiy Komsomolets[139] admits he is astonished when he hears Julia and Lena singing live for the whole of the concert which is world class, and accompanied by a band of the highest standard. Gasparyan blames Shapovalov for his handling of the early t.A.T.u. shows and for making them sing at Eurovision like 'two soaked chikens' when they were capable of performances like the one they gave in St. Petersburg, which according to the journalist represents their 'second birth.'

As soon as they achieve this success in St. Petersburg t.A.T.u. return to prominence in the press: in an interview published in the magazine Bravo[140], Julia unexpectedly admits to having a relationship with Topalov Vladik, her ex boyfriend at Neposedi, who was half of the duo Smash! along with Sergey Lazarev until a few months ago.

The news spreads instantly on TV and in other magazines such as Pravda.ru[141] and Zhizn[142] to which Julia reveals she wants to have Vlad's child, and he in turn confirms the rumours in Komsomolskaya Pravda[143] of his impending marriage with Julia in the summer.

On 17th May Julia and Lena take part in the 'Details' programme live on STS. The girls appear confident and relaxed: once again

---

[139] Arthur Gasparyan, " 'ТАТУ' не смогли собрать СКК в Питере", Moskovskiy Komsomolets, 5 May 2006.

[140] "Сенсация: Юля встречается с Владом Топаловым!" BRAVO! Russia no. 17, April 2006.

[141] Guerman Grachev, TATU girls unfazed by the Duma refusal to award them state decoration, Pravda.ru, 17 May 2006.

[142] Влад Топалов удочерит дочку Юли Волковой, Newsmusic.ru, 3 May 2006.

[143] Mary Remizova "ТАТУШКА Юля Волкова выходит замуж за Влада Топалова", Komsomolskaya Pravda, 18 May 2006.

they tackle the issue of the split with Shapovalov, speaking with respect and gratitude for their mentor, but at the same time asserting that they are now adults and want to take total control of their own future as artists. They confirm that they actively participate in the choice of music together with their staff and take care of vocal production in the tracks in Russian (responsibility for the English language versions is obviously left entirely to Interscope). The girls end by clarifying once again the meaning of the lyrics of *Lyudi Invalidy*, which is still causing concern among right-minded people.

A big concert is planned for 29th May in Mongolia at the 40,000-seat Central Sports Arena in the capital Ulan Bator. The concert is cancelled, however: the local organising committee could not guarantee that the Sports Arena would be used as the venue as it was temporarily unavailable, and t.A.T.u.'s management would not accept the proposed alternative venue because it was smaller.

On 2nd June t.A.T.u. are awarded three prizes at the MUZ TV Awards: Best Group, Best Video and Best Song of the year. During the ceremony which is broadcast live on the music channel, Julia and Lena perform *All About Us* and *Nas Ne Dogonyat* live with the full band to a cheering audience. The last song, which is from the group's early days, is actually sung mainly by the audience: Julia sings only the main parts and avoids the high-pitched chorus, and in fact it is Lena who ventures to sing (just once) Julia's falsetto part. In spite of this the performance goes down particularly well thanks to the band's input and - exactly in line with t.A.T.u.'s new style - is closer to that of a rock band than the old pop duo.

Their performance at the Pennenzakkenrock music event in Belgium is right at the other end of the spectrum though; the concert is organised for Flemish school children and is held at the end of the school year. A group of such international renown as t.A.T.u. are completely out of place in a concert like this, which although attracting an audience of thousands of youngsters, features artists that are almost exclusively local bands and singers unknown outside Holland and Belgium. To see Julia and Lena performing at 2 o'clock on a summer's afternoon with the entire band at what seems more like a summer camp than a rock concert, must have been quite something for any actual fans of t.A.T.u. who were there. Sven confesses he was a little ashamed to be playing in such a place in front of friends and relatives who'd come from Germany to hear him play.

At the end of the month the news goes out that *Loves Me Not* will be the fourth single from the album *Dangerous & Moving*; Julia reveals in her online journal that the video is due to be filmed in July, but the plans are soon changed.

In mid-July t.A.T.u. are in Mexico for a short promotional tour and two concerts. The first is at the Palacio De Los Deportes in Mexico City which is sold out (slightly under 10,000 tickets) a week before the event. Julia and Lena are very popular in Mexico, and there is further proof of this in Guadalahara where the second concert is held at the Vincente Ferndandez Arena. It goes so well that in the middle of *All The Thing She Said* the girls actually exchange a brief kiss on the lips on stage for the first time in a very long time, although it's only fleeting.

The next day there is to be an autograph-signing at the biggest music store in the city, Mr. CD. Hundreds more people turn up than expected and the security arrangements are totally inadequate for such a huge mass of cheering fans; when Julia and Lena arrive they rush towards the small platform set up for the girls instead of waiting in an orderly queue, and the girls only manage reach the platform with great difficulty and are visibly frightened. The situation becomes perilous for both the public and for Lena and Julia, so only twenty minutes into the session, which was due to go on for a couple of hours, and as soon as the security service manages to make a passage through the crowd with the help of some volunteers, the girls literally run away, to the huge disappointment of those waiting, some of whom have been queuing for several hours just to get a CD autographed.

Before returning home to Russia and after a series of meetings with the local press, t.A.T.u. are guests of the most popular live programme on Mexican TV, 'L'Otro Rollo', where they perform *All The Thing She Said, Dangerous & Moving* and *Loves Me Not* live with the band.

During the month of July, t.A.T.u.'s management finalise the schedule for the *Dangerous & Moving Tour* in Russia and Ukraine, with twenty-four dates between August and November. At the same time Julia and Lena carry out a mini tour of Japan to promote the DVD *Truth*, and perform at a big concert in the Korean capital Seoul, but some of these gigs eventually fall through.

Also in July, Julia is back in the gossip columns again for another alleged pregnancy. The rumours are immediately denied by the management, but the scandal magazine Zhizn[144] claims a month later that Volkova had lost the baby in her third month.

On 28th July Julia and Lena are in Helsinki, Finland, where they perform live at the Race & Rock Festival. A few days later Universal announce the forthcoming release in September of the album *The Best,* containing tracks from t.A.T.u.'s first two albums, *Ne Ver', Ne Bojsja* (the Eurovision song), *Null And Void* (unreleased version of *Objeznka Nol* in English) and a few remixes. The English version of *Prostiye Dvizheniya*, A Simple Motion, is also announced as one of the tracks on the album, but this song is dropped from the final version. The album is also released with an accompanying DVD containing the latest videos (including the animated version of *Gomenasai)* and some live tracks performed at Glam As You Party in Paris in 2005. The announcement of the album leaves fans stunned: greatest hits albums normally come out after a group's third or fourth album,

---

[144] *Юля Волкова потеряла ребенка от неизвестного отца,* Newsmusic.ru, 15 August 2006.

and *The Best* doesn't even contain any unpublished tracks that could justify it. But they only have to wait until the end of August before they get the answer to this understandable confusion.

Meanwhile, Julia and Lena have been in the Russian Black Sea resort of Sochi since early August. The days leading up to 4th August (the date of their first official gig of the *Dangerous & Moving* tour) have clearly been sunny because when Julia walks on stage she has a conspicuous tan, which stands out even more in contrast to Lena's fair skin. The audience are very relaxed and there's a great atmosphere in the house, so the concert is very laid back and the girls interact with the audience and make little jokes between songs.

Eleven days later t.A.T.u. return to Japan after nearly a year's absence to promote the release of the DVD *Truth*, which has been postponed by a month. Within their first forty-eight hours in Tokyo Julia and Lena give interviews, open a fireworks exhibition, perform at Club Addict and record a radio broadcast. On 18th August they're expected in Nagoya, where after a few meetings with the press, radio and TV, three short performances are planned in three different parts of the city. The timing doesn't seem particularly well thought out though, and when Julia and Lena's car arrives at Club Holiday around 10.30pm they're told that the club is still half-empty. Since the other two performances are scheduled to start soon after, the management decides to proceed straight the other two venues. The cancellation of the first performance, which is only announced after the band had already started rehearsing in front of the few people who were there, gets wide coverage in the press the next day[145]. The Japanese reporters haven't forgotten what happened in the Asahi TV studios in 2003 and they don't think it's very loyal of the two Russian singers who are so popular in Japan to suddenly run out again. The prominence that the press give to this incident obliges Neformat Japan, who look after

---

[145] タトゥーまた*ドタキャン!?Nikkan Sports*, 19 August 2006.

t.A.T.u.'s interests in Japan, to issue a statement in which they say that the decision to cancel the show was agreed with the manager of the club and that negotiations with the latter allowed t.A.T.u. certain discretions if the event was inadequately promoted. The rest of the Japanese promotional tour in Tokyo, Yokohama, Sapporo and Hokkaido goes without further hitch. From Hokkaido Julia and Lena were meant to fly straight to Yuzhno-Sakhalinsk where the second *D&M* tour was due to take place, but the entire batch of performances scheduled for the last week in August in Nakhodka, Vladivostok and Khabarovsk have also been cancelled in the interim. The first official announcement cites reasons of expediency following the plane crash in Donetsk on 22nd August with170 casualties, but rumours about cancelling the tour had already started in Eastern Russia two days before the disaster, when the group were in Japan. Tatuism, it seems, is effectively still part and parcel of t.A.T.u. even when they're light years away from Shapovalov: between late August and early September the latest in a series of misadventures takes its toll on their short history. On 31st August a brief statement[146] announces the mutually agreed dissolution of the contract that binds t.A.T.u. to Universal International. Despite the routine mutual thanks expressed in the official press release, the press[147] try to find out the reasons for the disagreement that has arisen lately between the group and the record label, speculating about excessive demands from t.A.T.u. for recording a new album and the videos for it. In the coming years the multimillion-dollar legal disputes between TA Music and Universal International Music BV will be taken up by many international law firms.

Whatever the reason that prompted the professional split, it is important to compare international sales results for *Dangerous & Moving* with those for *200 Km/h In The Wrong Lane*: the

---

[146] *t.A.T.u. расстались с Universal,* Vazhno.ru, 31 August 2006.

[147] Utro.ru, 15 September 2006.

latter sold almost two million copies in Japan alone and a total of around 5 million worldwide, whilst the 2006 album didn't even reach one million, including every country where it was on sale. The difference is even more striking when you consider that sales in the United States, where t.A.T.u.'s first album sold a little under 900,000 copies, the second album sold just over a tenth of that figure[148].

In relation to these results, Universal International had invested much more on production of the second album than it did on the first: Julia and Lena stayed a full six months in Los Angeles to record it and writers, artists and high level professional technicians were brought in; the videos produced in the USA were much more sophisticated and costly to produce than the ones Shapovalov produced in his era in Russia. The resulting album was decidedly more structured, mature and sophisticated, but wasn't as successful as was hoped.

But to make any meaningful comparison statistics you also have to take market trends into account. The first decade of the twenty-first century was devastating for the global music industry: the advent of downloadable music and file sharing and the generational change in habits of the main consumers led to a downturn in the industry. As far back as 2002 when *200 Km/h In The Wrong Lane* was released, the ten best-selling albums worldwide totalled only 33.5 million copies, exactly half of what was sold two years earlier[149]. In view of this it would be unthinkable three years on to achieve the same results as for the first album, and Universal would have perhaps been celebrating if they'd exceeded two and a half million sales for *Dangerous & Moving*; the problem is that they didn't sell even half that number, and the record label probably didn't even break even. Just like their initial success, this

---

[148] Gary Trust, *Ask Billboard: "Taking Peaks," Nos.100-1,* Billboard.com, 29 January 2010.

[149] Christopher M. Wright, *"In search of the lost chord,",* *The Financial Manager,* October-December 2003.

partial debacle of t.A.T.u. is likewise the result of a combination of various causes. The first is undoubtedly that they no longer have that phenomenal driving force of a controversial and shocking image that first propelled Julia and Lena onto TV screens, newspapers and radio stations across the world. The second is their tender age: as we have already had occasion to witness, although t.A.T.u. do not belong to the so-called teen pop genre, teenage followers (who make up just 18% of the CD market in the West[150]) saw themselves reflected in the two carefree and rebellious schoolgirls that Shapovalov created, while the target audience of the vaguely rock-oriented *Dangerous & Moving* t.A.T.u. are apparently no longer in the 13 to 17 age group. The shift is inevitable because time moves on for Julia and Lena as it does for everyone and they are now older. The one thing that was not expected, if anything, is that many of the fans who were 13 years old in 2003 would abandon t.A.T.u. in 2006: the inverse coming-out and the change of image in 2004 would obviously have disappointed a large section of their audience. Lena says in an interview with Cosmopolitan[151] (Ukrainian edition):

> With the second album our audience expanded in a qualitative sense, but we lost some of our fans. Why? Probably because they were mainly interested in the story of the two girls and weren't that keen on their music. (Lena Katina, 2006)

Let's not forget too that t.A.T.u.'s unfamiliarity with western show business rules was a highly distinctive characteristic for them which gave them a competitive edge, and the belated confession that the personal relationship between them was just fiction undoubtedly had an enormously detrimental effect on its appeal.

---

[150] Ed Christman, *New Life for CDs* - Billboard.biz, 1 April 2006.

[151] Victoria Gordienko *"Группа ТАТУ. Две стихии", Cosmopolitan Ukraine,* January 2007.

Finally, the marketing for *Dangerous & Moving* inexplicably appears to have been much less effective than that for *200 Km/h:* just consider how the USA was virtually excluded from any direct promotional activities. It's true that other countries such as those in South America were targetted, but it's also true that almost a third of the entire global music market[152] is monopolised by the USA, followed by Japan (one fifth); South American countries represent a much smaller share of the sales, and commercially it would be impossible for anyone to compensate for the loss of the US market even with more than excellent results in South America.

But notwithstanding all these valid considerations, the main factor is time. And Shapovalov's words at the famous meeting in Moscow in early 2003 now seem prophetic:

> Singers cannot remain at their peak of worldwide fame for very long: if we fail to maintain global media exposure today, it will be completely useless tomorrow. The world does not need us. (Ivan Shapovalov, 2003)

If we analyse the careers of young artists who made their debut in the same period, we find that Pink released her second album nineteen months after the first, Britney Spears after sixteen months, Christina Aguilera after just thirteen, and t.A.T.u. after thirty-four long months. Three years is a long time in itself, but it's an eternity when you consider the age of Julia and Lena's fans; between thirteen and sixteen a teenager's life changes radically: they go from being little more than children to being young adults. Their musical tastes change as do their idols if you don't give them enough encouragement to go on, and Shapovalov - being the good psychologist that he was - knew all this.

---

[152] IFPI - IULM *Economy of Music,* Report 2009 (reference year 2007).

ALONE AGAINST THE WORLD

It wasn't hard to work out that the collaboration between Universal Music International and TA Music had come to the end of the line several months before it was officially announced: with repeated delays in the release of the DVD *Truth* and the sudden release of the CD *The Best* it became abundantly clear. Before the official break with t.A.T.u. Universal tried to recoup as much as possible of their investment in the group by staking everything on an album with virtually no outlay (the songs, including *Null And Void,* were already available), that was bound to sell a fair number of copies, and the results bear this out.

From September 2006, TA Music which was created to take care of production in Russia following the split with Shapovalov, and which counted Lena and Julia[153] amongst its shareholders, becomes t.A.T.u.'s own independent label. 'Battleship Тату' no longer has any protection, not even from the international power of Universal, and the rust of decline is starting to corrode the supporting structure. From this point on the girls have only their music to fall back on to determine their future in the business.

Under these conditions other pop stars would have broken down, either mentally or professionally, but not them. Julia and Lena are not so different from those girls who screamed 'this is my music!' seven years ago. They may no longer have their youthful enthusiasm, but their naivety is essentially the same as it was, as much as it can be after having lived for several years at the

---

[153] Boris Barabanov *"Юлия Волкова: хотим Красную площадь"*, *Kommersant*, no.3289, 31 October 2005.

pinnacle of fame in their own country and with massive exposure in the rest of the world; of course, Julia and Lena don't live like just any two 20-something students in Moscow, but neither do they go around with a posse of bodyguards, a miniature dog under their arms and trailing a personal hairdresser, as happens often with American pop stars at the peak of their success. Sergei Lavrov, who organised many of t.A.T.u.'s concerts in Russia, agrees, in an interview with Gazeta Express[154]:

> They stayed just as they were: simple, open, with no pop star attitude. They still share a double room when they stay in hotels, they're patient if the air conditioning is not working in the car, and if they have to walk from the hotel to where they're going, it's no problem for them. (Sergei Lavrov, 2006)

So t.A.T.u. don't just dissolve; a brief statement on their official website confirms this on 31st August, announcing that activities are continuing, that a new album will be released in 2007 and that the whole band - referred to as indispensible - is staying with them. 'What we need to decide now is how, with whom and above all, which way to go,' says the announcement, 'but all the key people are staying with us.'

The fact that Sven, Troy, Steve and Domen are staying in the group will safeguard the future of the *Dangerous & Moving Tour* and this is critical to the economic livelihood of t.A.T.u., but after the recording debacle other problems now arise with the live performances. A statement issued on 7 September following a concert in Samara announces the cessation of the partnership between t.A.T.u. and Kreml. Consert: organisers of some of the events planned for the tour, and so the calendar has to be amended accordingly.

---

[154] Mikhail Filimonov *"Бойфренд ТАТУШЕК "ПОДАЛ в суд на их нового продюсера"*, *Express Gazeta*, 29 September 2006

The decision immediately triggers a controversy in the press[155]: on one hand Kreml. Consert argues that t.A.T.u. are unable to attract a big enough audience even to cover costs, and that the concerts in Samara (September 2) and Kaliningrad (September 9) took place in front of just a few thousand people; Zhenya Voevodina, the group's press officer, on the other hand, argues that the problem with Kreml. Consert is of a purely contractual nature.

> The problems on the Russian part of the tour were caused mainly by the local organisers. Payments were often not made, concerts were not promoted adequately and so on. The groups in Western Europe didn't work this way: it was a difficult tour - it would have been much simpler in the West. Unfortunately we didn't have a permanent agent in Europe, we were outside of European show business. (Sven Martin, 2012)

While their management try to reorganise the tour stops at home, Julia and Lena fly to Seoul with the band to perform at the festival of Russian culture being held in the South Korean capital. This is the first ever t.A.T.u. gig in Korea, and the event draws a lot of attention from the public and from the local press[156]. The concert at the Olympic Hall is a success: Julia and Lena follow the usual *Dangerous & Moving Tour* programme, but this time during *Gomenasai* they turn and hug and kiss each other on the lips, although it's more playful than sensual. Images of the kiss are reproduced the next day on all Korean broadcasting networks.

On 21st September *All About Us* wins the award for Best Video of the Year at the MTV Russian Music Awards, but Julia and Lena do not attend the ceremony in St. Petersburg. The reason was explained a few days earlier during a press conference in Seoul by

---

[155] *Гастрольный тур "ТАТУ по России проваливается со скандалом"*, Newsmusic.ru, 12 September 2006.
[156] Chung Ah-young *"Russian duo to hold 1st concert"*, The Korea Times, 18 September 2006.

Julia herself: the organisers were not planning a performance by t.A.T.u. as part of the show, and she and Lena were not interested in being there just as guests[157].

The next day though the girls attend a ceremony at the Theatre of Mossovet in Moscow for presentation of the GQ Awards. Julia and Lena are named 'Women of the Year 2006' by the popular men's magazine as and perform *Polchasa* live, accompanied by their keyboardist Sven Martin. At the end of the song Julia, turning towards Lena, replaces the last repetition of the word *'polchasa'* with the phrase *'ya Tvoya'* (I'm yours).

At the end of the month Julia and Lena are guests on the TV show '100 Questions to an Adult'[158] (recorded few weeks in advance), where they are called on to answer questions from an audience of teenagers. Sitting on couches in the studio, surrounded by girls and boys the same age as they were when they made their public debut in 2000 as t.A.T.u., Julia and Lena seem light years away from the days of Shapovalov's schoolgirls. But the teenagers present, who were barely out of elementary school six years ago, and probably didn't even understand the words to the songs, still imagined them to be 15-years-olds. Because Julia and Lena are holding hands, they start asking them about their relationship with each other: Julia puts herself in their place and tells them what she would have told them six years ago: 'I love her.' Lena smiles, but as always manages to remain unruffled when she is asked if she feels the same way about Julia, and replies slightly awkwardly, 'of course.' Young people can be a lot more direct than many journalists though, and shortly afterwards one girl presses Julia again, 'what did you mean exactly when you said you love her?' and at this point Lena is forced to intervene, saying, 'It's a figure of speech. It was a joke, but not everyone gets it all the time.' Once again in this

---

[157] *"ТАТУ: UNIVERSAL заработал на нас бешеные деньги. Это кончилось!"*, Newsmusic.ru, 19 September 2006.
[158] *100 вопросов к взрослому*, TVC, 30 September 2006.

period of great uncertainty for their professional future, Julia and Lena seem to be prisoners of their past; a past they can't deny because it's what led them to success, but a past they can't resurrect either. The most attentive observers notice this, and in the aforementioned article in Cosmopolitan the interviewer asks Julia why in recent concerts she sometimes goes back to the behaviour she displayed in t.A.T.u.'s early days; touching Lena's breasts or buttocks:

> It's not a theatrical ploy, these are instinctive gestures. I'm attracted to both men and women. [...] Love for a woman and love for a man stimulate completely different feelings, and I've never denied that I appreciate both. (Julia Volkova, 2006)

On 2nd October t.A.T.u. are in Kazan, in the Russian republic of Tatarstan, where they hold a press conference and a concert.

October 4 is Lena's 22nd birthday. In her online journal she writes that she doesn't feel like organising a proper party: they're meeting up at a restaurant near where the group are based in Moscow for the evening; there'll be Lena's family, the band and the other t.A.T.u. staff members. It turns out to be a very pleasant dinner though, and Julia gives Lena a pair of precious diamond earrings as a present.

The *Dangerous & Moving Tour* then moves on to Ukraine; in Kiev Julia and Lena perform first at the Freedom Hall in front of a select group, then at a large concert at the Sport Palace, and finally at Dnepropetrovsk.

Meanwhile, whilst the album *The Best* makes its debut in Taiwan and reaches the top spot in the sales rankings, Julia reveals in an interview with Radio Russia Kiev that they are due to start filming in early 2007 for a movie with t.A.T.u. in the leading role. The film, to be made by a well-known American director, will be based

131

on a novella entitled 't.A.T.u. Come Back', by Alexey Mitrofanov and Anastasia Moiseeva.

Moiseeva is a history of art student at the Russian State University of Humanities, and Mitrofanov is a 40-year-old Member of the National Liberal Democratic Party in the State Duma (the lower house of the Russian Federal Assembly), a film buff and well-known fan of t.A.T.u. and of Volkova in particular. Julia had met him for the first time the previous year at the launch of a new women's magazine. Since then they had met on various occasions and Mitrofanov was undisguisedly supportive of the group in many interviews[159], finally proposing[160] Julia and Lena as recipients of the Order of Friendship in November 2005, which is awarded to those who have made a substantial contribution to Russia in establishing bonds of friendship with other peoples (the proposal was later rejected by the committee).

t.A.T.u. Come Back is a story told through a series of text messages of a relationship between two girls who, after becoming friends over the internet, finally meet in person at a t.A.T.u. concert in Moscow's Gaudi Arena, and is based on a true story. It's not a book about t.A.T.u. per se, who only appear in the background, but nevertheless when Julia announces the film it is regarded as the Volkova-Katina film debut for some time to come.

With a few setbacks (cancellation of the concert in Perm for unspecified technical problems) the *Dangerous & Moving Tour* continues in Kirov, Yekaterinburg, Volgograd, Ufa, and later in Siberia at Surgut and Novosibirsk with great success in terms of audiences and reviews.

You never knew what would happen at these gigs. The facilities were inadequate and the further east we went the worse it got:

---

[159] *Митрофанов любит "ТАТУ, а ЛДПР "сотрудничает" со многими группами",* Newsmusic.ru, 29 April 2005.

[160] *Lawmaker Proposes state honors for pop duo Tatu,* RIA Novosti, 15 November 2005.

the stage, the power lines, the electricity supply. You had to be ready for any unforeseen hitch. (Sven Martin, 2012)

13th November is planned as the broadcast date for the first of a new reality series on MUZ TV called Travel Party, shot during t.A.T.u.'s tour of Japan the previous August, but the programme is removed from the schedule at the last minute and postponed to a later date, to be confirmed. It is never reinstated, and rumours about its release on DVD prove to be unfounded.

On November 14, t.A.T.u. are in Irkutsk on the last leg of the Siberian tour; two days later they are in the Armenian capital of Yerevan, and finally on November 19 they close this part of the *Dangerous & Moving Tour* with a concert in Yaroslav, Russia.

Back at home, t.A.T.u. are now confronted with the *Lyudi Invalidy* issue: Leonid Vokuyev, Head of the Committee for Human Rights of the Russian republic of Komi, publicly declares[161] his intention to prosecute the group t.A.T.u. through the Moscow Prosecutor's Office for contempt against people with disabilities, in respect of the phrase contained in the booklet attached to the album, which reads:

Disabled people are born that way and will die that way. They don't know what it means to be human. They're just imitations, based on the anthropoid model. They have legs, hands and other body parts; physically, they are indistinguishable from humans. But people with disabilities don't live, they just function. Their actions are laid down by the laws of mechanics and have four settings: cruelty, stupidity, greed, meanness. Everything they do is operational, predictable, weak, and destructive. All bad things that happen, very bad, ugly things, are caused by the actions of people with disabilities.

---

[161] *"Уполномоченный по правам человека в Коми: последний диск ГРУППЫ 'ТАТУ'"*, IA *Regnum*, 17 November 2006.

The news causes quite a stir in Russia and Julia and Lena are invited onto numerous radio and television shows to express their views on the matter. Through the microphones of BBC Radio Russia[162] Lena explains:

The title *Lyudi Invalidy* could be interpreted the wrong way, but there's no way the explanation referred to can possibly be interpreted ambiguously. It obviously refers to moral invalids, people who have no human soul or feelings. [...] We have great respect for the disabled and we're always careful to reserve special seating for them at our concerts; we meet them and we have our photos taken with them.

Julia and Lena also reaffirm their position on the TV show 'Let them Speak' on Channel One Russia; Alexey Mitrofanov and Sergey Lazarev also join the debate in defence of t.A.T.u. After a lot of hype it turns out to be a storm in a teacup: nothing more is heard about the alleged legal action over the months that follow.
Meanwhile 2006 ends for Lena and Julia with four performances, the first two at venues in Moscow: the Prado Cafe and the B1 Club, the third at the Siemens Arena in Vilnius and the last one on 20th December at the People Club in Chisinau. They celebrate New Year separately; Julia spends it with little Vika and other family members and Lena is with her family at first and later with her old school friends.
The January 2007 edition of Ukrainian Cosmopolitan magazine[163] publishes an extended article on t.A.T.u. Lena gives the journalist a hard-hitting description of how she and Lena complement each other perfectly:

---

[162] *Morning on BBC show*, 24 November 2006.

[163] Victoria Gordienko, *"ГРУППА 'ТАТУ'.Две стихии"*, *Cosmopolitan Ukraine*, January 2007.

Julia is a very determined person who keeps to the path she's set for herself and never looks back. I'm more of a worrier, I'm afraid of new situations, of what could happen if things don't go the way you expect. At times like these Julia tells me, 'calm down, everything will be fine.' She's always upbeat and manages to cheer me up and make me think that things are not so bad really. We are completely different people: if you could take what's good from each of us you'd probably end up with the perfect woman.

And to the question about why she loves Lena, Julia answers:

Because she's there: she's a sister, a friend, a mother, a girlfriend, a woman, all at the same time. We're very different and we complement each other.

BELIY PLASCHIK

The first rumours about the film starring t.A.T.u., provisionally entitled Tatu Come Back, appear in the press in January 2007: shooting is expected to start in the spring and the production house will be the Russian American Movie Company according to the Russian edition of Forbes.

Julia and Lena are in Germany at this time together with Sven Martin to record the first demos of songs for the new album. The earliest versions of *Ne Zhaley, You and I* and *Beliy Plaschik* are recorded in this period, and they work on *Running Blind* at the Record Bay studios in Mönchengladbach, where this song was composed some time earlier by Sven and Julian Schramm.

The group's objective at the moment is to produce an album with less challenging content than the last one. Julia says as much when she returns to Moscow in February, in an interview with MK.ru magazine[164], in which she announces that the actual recordings should begin in Los Angeles in March. A few months later, however,[165] Lena defines the new album as a sort of continuation of *Lyudi Invalidy*.

In early February Julia once again becomes a target for the tabloid press over the alleged excesses of her ex-boyfriend Vlad towards herself and her new partner Parviz[166]. The only response Julia makes is to give herself a two-week break in Thailand, far away from Moscow and the whole controversy, with her new fiancé,

---

[164] *"ТАТУ" Нас просто прет от живого звука!,* Newsmusic.ru, 6 February 2007.

[165] *"t.A. T. и.: 'Ну Миша...Ну, Бартон'",* Elle Girl Russia, December 2007.

[166] *"ТАТУ ШКУ" Юлю обвиняют в наркомании,* News@mail.ru, 16 February 2007.

where she also celebrates her 22nd birthday. Lena sends her very affectionate greetings publicly through her blog, wishing her well and restating her affection for her:

> I will always be beside you, no matter what happens. (Lena Katina, 2007)

When February rolls into March t.A.T.u.'s management confirm that Roland Joffé is to be the director of the film about the group, and rumours that were circulating some time ago[167] about a supposed collaboration with Stacey Ann Ferguson (Fergie) of the Black Eyes Peas are repudiated.

In Moscow Julia is now frequently seen at social events in the company of young businessman Parviz Yasinov, and the local press waste no time circulating rumours of a forthcoming wedding. As her new boyfriend is Muslim and already married with children, the rumour[168] is spread that Julia may convert to Islam in order to become his second wife, since polygamy is permitted under Islam.

March 16 is the birthday of the Deputy, Alexey Mitrofanov, one of t.A.T.u.'s most ardent fans, and Julia and Lena are invited to the party; Julia is there, of course, with Parviz.

The following day t.A.T.u. fly with the whole band to Venice to entertain 250 guests, along with Tiziano Ferro, at the lavish[169] birthday party that 'king of vodka' Roustam Tariko - one of the richest men in the world - has organised at the prestigious Giorgio Cini Foundation on the island of St. George.

The following week an episode of 'Closer to the Stars' goes out on MUZ TV, with t.A.T.u. as the subjects, and more details about the film are revealed, for which shooting is about to commence and

---

[167] *"Тату" споют с Ферджи*, News@mail.ru, 14 February 2007.

[168] *"ТАТУШКА" Юля попала в гарем*, News@mail.ru, 15 March 2007.

[169] МН, *"I due volti dell'est: sfarzo russo, miseria moldova"*, L'Espresso, 19 March 2007.

proceed for a few months. The author of the book, Mitrofanov, confirms that it is inspired by the true story of two female fans of t.A.T.u. intending to run away together to Moscow. During a quarrel that arises when they try to get their ID papers from their parents, the mother of one of them is accidentally killed. The girls end up in jail and ask if they can serve their sentences in the same cell, where they still are today. In the interview, Julia says she believes it will be a movie full of scandal and outrage in true t.A.T.u. style, and that she and Lena will be playing themselves.

In April, whilst Julia and Lena are in Los Angeles to continue recording the new album, it is announced that t.A.T.u. will be giving a concert on May 3 in the Egyptian resort of Sharm el-Sheikh. A few days before the scheduled date, however, the concert is postponed to a later date: they actually perform at the famous coastal resort just a year later.

On April 24, the book *PodNeBesy* by Katya Ledokol is released[170]. The title deliberately references the reality show 'Podnebesnaya' of 2004, a few months before which the author claims to have been sent by Ivan Shapovalov to follow Julia and Lena's everywhere and monitor their movements in anticipation of their expected 'mutiny'. According to Ledokol's (heavily fictionalised) version[171] Julia and Lena deliberately changed their public image from 2003 to provoke the split from Shapovalov, but their romantic relationship was genuine and not simulated. As confirmation of this - according to the author - the lyrics for *Loves Me Not* were inspired by the affair when Julia was engaged to a man and became pregnant by him, and left him after she realised she'd lost the most important thing she had - Lena. The release of Ledokol's book sends a few ripples around the forums from t.A.T.u. fans, but doesn't trigger any significant backlash from Julia and Lena.

---

[170] Katya Ledokol, *PodNeBesy*, Iauza-Press 2007.

[171] *t.A.T.u. zawsze śpią razem*, *Interia.pl*, 30 April 2007.

May 27 is the day scheduled for Gay Pride in Moscow. The event was banned by the mayor of the Russian capital the year before, and once again in 2007 the authorities seem determined to refuse permission for the parade. On 17th May Julia and Lena whilst in Los Angeles decide to issue a message,[172] in which they declare their support for those who defend free choice of sexual orientation and reaffirm that they have never purposefully betrayed the trust of their fans of any sexual orientation throughout their career. The girls conclude by saying they intend to do everything possible to attend the parade in Moscow later that month. Julia and Lena keep their promise and are present at a press conference on the 26th (at which Alexey Mitrofanov is also present) to announce that there will be a demonstration against the ban on the gay parade by the city authorities, to be held the next day in Tverskaya Ulitsa. Hundreds of activists are expected to turn up at the allotted time the next morning, but when Julia and Lena arrive they find only about 50[173], amongst which are the Italian deputy Vladimir Luxuria, MEP Marco Cappato and other members of the Italian Radical Party. The group of protesters is attacked by a group of skinheads despite police presence, and the girls, who are immediately removed to a safe distance by members of their team, watch the scene and even offer refuge[174] in their luxury tour bus. The next day in an interview with the Italian newspaper La Repubblica[175], Julia tells how she is shocked that her city, Moscow, has demonstrated itself to be an uncivilised city on this occasion, where people are afraid to take to the streets to declare their freedom.

---

[172] Arina Morokova, *"Группа t.A.T.и. готова прервать работу над новым альбом"*, *NR2 New Russia*, 17 May 2007.

[173] *Gay Pride a Mosca, aggrediti i radicali Picchiata anche Vladimir Luxuria*, La Repubblica.it, 27 May 2007.

[174] "Gay Pride: Luxuria salvata da gruppo lesbo russo", *AGI*, 28 May 2007.

[175] Leonardo Coen, *"Noi russi con la paura di andare in piazza così l'Occidente resta un sogno lontano"*, *La Repubblica*, 29 May 2007.

While she's in Moscow the American actress Mischa Barton, who is to play one of the two lead parts in the film, tries to familiarise herself with the Russian capital in preparation for the start of filming; in early June rumours that Volkova is once again pregnant are confirmed. As the magazine Tvoi Den[176] reveals, Julia, already in her third month, is happy to give Parviz a child, and her only concern is how his wife, Masha Veber (a former singer herself) will react to the news.

On June 24 t.A.T.u. are expected as the main performing artists at the Zvukovaya Dorozhka MK Festival scheduled at the outdoor Luzhniki sports complex in Moscow, involving the participation of several other national pop stars such as Serebro and Dima Bilan. The news of Julia's pregnancy worries the organisers and also t.A.T.u. fans, who are hoping to hear one of the songs from the album that they're currently recording at the Los Angeles studios, but Julia herself reassures everyone through the pages of MK.ru[177] saying:

This is not my first pregnancy and I know what to do. I'm in good shape and I plan to go on performing at least until the end of October.

And t.A.T.u. do in fact appear on stage at the festival as expected, performing *Lyudi Invalidy, All About Us, Loves Me Not, Ne Ver Ne Boisya, Ne Prosi, Nas Ne Dogonyat* and a song taken from the new album for the first time. This song is *Ne Zhaley,* a poignant ballad that, according to Lena, made her mother cry the first time she heard it.

Although Lena claims to be delighted about Julia's new pregnancy in her online journal, the press imply after the exhibition in Moscow that Katina is greatly annoyed at having to bring t.A.T.u.'s artistic activities to a halt once again because of a situation

---

[176] *"Юля Волкова: Я беременна!", Tvoi Den,* no.227, 6 June 2007.

[177] *"Юля Волкова: 'Я беременна, но это временно'", Moskovskiy Komsomolets,* 22 June 2007.

imposed by her alter-ego. According to reports by Alena Mazhorova in the magazine Zhizn[178], Lena arrives backstage alone, exchanges just a few essential words with Julia and after the show deliberately ignores her.

Whether or not these rumours are true, the fact is that Volkova's second pregnancy has fallen at a very inopportune moment for t.A.T.u.'s career, after clawing their way back into the limelight with enormous difficulty in 2005 from an extended absence necessitated initially by Julia's voice problems and then by her first pregnancy (as well as the crisis with Shapovalov); battleship Тату now seems doomed to sink for good. From this perspective, the tears that Inessa Katina cried for *Ne Zhaley* would seem to bestow upon the following verses of this beautiful song an autobiographical interpretation:

> *My s toboi molchim* You and I remain silent
> *Ty I Ya vdvoyom* You and I together
> *Dal'she hotim* We don't want to go on
> *Bol'she poyom* We are not singing anymore

But it's not necessarily Julia's pregnancy that convinces t.A.T.u. that their artistic journey together is coming to an end: *Ne Zhaley* was written before Volkova became pregnant. The fact remains that even to this day, the lyrics do seem like a valediction from those who already know that this will be t.A.T.u.'s last album.

At the end of June come conflicting reports about what stage of development the new album is at: on one hand Lena answers questions from fans in her online journal saying that the album is almost ready, but on the other hand statements[179] are drawn from the band's guitarist, Troy McCubbin, who claims he still knows very little about the new songs and that in fact nothing has been

---

[178] Alena Mazhorova, *"ТА не понимает ТУ"*, Zhizn, 27 June 2007.
[179] *Третий альбом 'ТАТУ' под вопросом*, META.ua, 3 July 2007.

recorded yet, in spite of the fact that Julia and Lena have been in Los Angeles for several months. The only definite thing - as revealed by MK.ru[180] - seems to be the title, *Upravlenie Otbrosami* (Waste Management). The motivation for the strange title is explained by the girls more than a year later in a radio interview[181]: during inspections for a video in the U.S. (probably the one for *Beliy Plaschik*) Julia and Lena had seen some elegant writing in white on a lush green lawn that said just that - Waste Management. The stark contrast between the surroundings and what the writing actually said piqued their imagination. The timings in this story, however, don't seem to match up, because by the time the *Beliy Plaschik* video is shot, the title of the new album has already been known for some time.

At the beginning of July Julia and Lena run the first scenes of the film (now with the new provisional title of *Finding tATu*) in the abandoned Badayevsky brewery. These are the final scenes, when Julia and Lena get the heroine, played by Mischa Barton, out of prison.

On 12 July, during an episode of Showbiz 'Obnazhenny' ('Naked Showbiz') on MUZ TV, focussing on Julia's recent love affairs with first Vlad and then Timati, a phrase uttered by Julia during an interview with journalist Yana Rudkovskaya and taken out of context, 'I've decided to think about a solo career', is immediately picked up by KP magazine[182] and becomes the subject of a short article under the unequivocal headline, 'Julia Volkova leaves t.A.T.u. for a solo career,' leaving t.A.T.u. fans worldwide in a panic. Julia personally denies the rumours at a press conference in Almaty, Kazakhstan[183].

---

[180] *"Юля Волкова: 'Я беременна, но это временно' ",* Moskovskiy Komsomolets, 22 June 2007.
[181] 7 премьеры, Radio 7 Moscow, 23 October 2008.
[182] Mary Remizova *"Юля Волкова уходит из 'ТАТУ' "*, Moskovskiy Komsomolets 12 July 2007.
[183] Margo Ervand *ТАТУАЛЬНЫЙ КОНТРОЛЬ*, Liter.kz, 19 July 2007.

With fans in Russia agitated, t.A.T.u. get top billing for the Planet of Music Festival in Astana, in advance of six dates of a music tour organised by Coca-Cola in Kazakhstan which will end on the 27th of the same month in Qaraghandy. In the city of Almaty t.A.T.u. have an unpleasant experience at the private party of middle-aged businessmen where they are asked to perform, incredibly, without any security presence or bodyguards. A few of the guests, inebriated and overexcited by the pretty girls in their costumes, as reported in an article in Zhizn magazine[184], start treating them like lap dancers in some dubious club, stuffing banknotes in Lena's pockets and Julia's boots, and grabbing at her leg to try to drag her off the stage. Volkova has to kick to break free from the grip of her hot-blooded admirer and bring the performance to a premature end. The press rumour is confirmed years later by Troy in his online blog[185].

Mishaps aside, the Coca-Cola Tour concerts are the first real performances of 2007, not including the private party in Venice and participation in the MK Festival. After the exhaustive 2006 tour t.A.T.u. have kept away from the stage for many months, and are feeling the effects of it. The Russian edition of Forbes monthly publication publishes a ranking of the 50 wealthiest performing stars in the country in its August issue, and t.A.T.u. are only placed at no.36, whereas they were at 6th place the year before. The ranking is compiled from box office takings, media presence and public interest in the artists in the period between 1st July 2006 and 30th June 2007. Within this period t.A.T.u. appear to have grossed only $1.4 million, while in the previous period they'd made $3.3. Julia and Lena, speaking to Russia Today cameras, claim to be not particularly surprised by the magazine's findings: 'We've done nothing in particular to get into the Forbes rankings, and frankly

---

[184] *"Беременную" ТАТУШКУ "пытались изнасиловать на закрытой вечеринке"*, *Tvoi Den*, 11 September 2007.
[185] troymaccubbin.fanbridge.com, fan questions, 25 February 2011.

we couldn't care less. All we know is we're the most famous Russian singers in the world.' Notwithstanding the girls' self-assuredness, their position in the Forbes ranking is a barometer of t.A.T.u.'s relentlessly plunging commercial potential: having already reported a significant reduction in sales of their second album and in their fanbase between 2005 and 2006, the delay in launching the new album, the absence of major performances in the last six months and their almost total disappearance from the international scene (the last appearance abroad dates back to Japan in August 2006) are increasingly eroding the already fragile plating on the formerly ponderous battleship Тату, which just a few years ago was collecting more platinum discs and international awards than they could count.

Time was never t.A.T.u.'s greatest ally, and once again it lives up to expectations: the ships sent to rescue the crew of the sinking battleship - the third album and the movie - arrive too late to save Julia and Lena and their fate is sealed.

But in August 2007 they're still unaware of what lies ahead, and they're working hard on the production of Finding t.A.T.u.: on the 15th Julia, Lena and the whole band hold a free concert at Club B1 in Moscow to shoot the final scene of the film, and perform *You and I* for the first time in public: the song that for the purposes of the story is written by the two heroines.

Because such short notice is given (the announcement was only made on the group's official website less than a week beforehand) the venue which has a capacity of 3,000 only manages to attract 500 fans. t.A.T.u.'s management are quick to point out that this was the required number, but nonetheless by judicious placing of people and cameras using the latest technology (the film is recorded digitally in HD), the director Joffé manages to give the impression that it's a sellout. Backstage, Julia takes a long time deciding what to wear on stage; first she tries a tee-shirt then takes it off, then asks Lena and Parviz for their opinions. Everyone advises her to wear the same old sleeveless bomber jacket that she wore in the *All About Us* video, and that she's worn many times on the *Dangerous & Moving Tour,* which reveals the blooming evidence of her pregnancy now in its fifth month, whilst Lena squeezes into a figure-hugging corset. At the concert - where Julia and Lena lip-sync to the song for the purposes of the film - the actresses Mischa Barton and Shantel Van Santen are also on the scene. As well as their best-loved songs, t.A.T.u. also perform a preview song taken from their next album, *Little People.*

Although after the B1 concert the number of unpublished songs already revealed to the public now total three, by late August the rest of the album is still all at sea: Sergio Galoyan says on his blog that he's suggested a good fifteen songs, of which four have been made into demos, but he still doesn't know which songs will actually be recorded. In the end Boris Rensky chooses just one of the Sergio's songs, who today remarks:

> The project was so far removed from its origins, it had become a rock group, it had lost every connection with what it stood for at the beginning. I seriously couldn't work with them on the third album because they wanted me to produce rock music, and by that time I'd realised that the right sound for t.A.T.u. was dance. (Sergio Galoyan, 2012)

Meanwhile, with filming finished - at least for them - Julia and Lena take a short break. Lena goes to Tuscany in Italy with her sister: they sunbathe on the beaches of Versilia in Viareggio and go to see La Bohème at the Puccini festival in Torre del Lago, then visit Florence, Pisa and Lucca. Julia and Parviz go to Cyprus in September for the sun and sea.

On 12th September, almost a year after the scheduled date, the long-awaited DVD, *Truth: Live in St. Petersburg* is finally released in Japan. The reasons for this colossal delay are the legal disputes between TA Music and Universal over the rights to some of the songs; in the end some songs performed at the concert are cut from the DVD and shown instead on TV: *Cosmos, Chto Ne Hvataet, Novaya Model* and *Polchasa.*

On 22nd September an episode of the investigative documentary 'USSR' focussing on t.A.T.u. is aired on Ren TV, in which Katya Ledokol is interviewed about the revelations contained in her book PodNeBesy.

Although she's in her sixth month of pregnancy, Julia subjects herself to the long return flight to Los Angeles in early October where the new video for *Beliy Plaschik* is being filmed: a pre-single from the new album with music composed by Vanya Kilar and lyrics inspired by three poems by Mary Maksakova, a sixteen-year-old student from St. Petersburg and a fan of t.A.T.u. who for more than a year has been posting her verses on the group's official forum under the name Eza.

Filming starts at 3pm on 6th October outside the Hyperion Treatment Plant, a wastewater treatment plant on the outskirts of Los Angeles. The area is heavily contaminated and the staff (about 30 people) have to take the necessary health & safety precautions. The result is without a doubt one of the most interesting music videos of recent years and it is directed, not surprisingly, by James Cox, who once again proves to have an uncommon creative harmony with t.A.T.u.

The video, which opens with the words 'one day in the 21st century,' tells the story of a young prisoner in an advanced state of pregnancy (Julia) on the eve of her execution, and the execution by a firing squad commanded by an Officer (Lena) who is a prostitute in her private life. At the shooting, where they fire dramatically just before a siren vainly sounds to alert them to stop the execution, a small crowd gathers to celebrate the occasion.

There have been many interpretations as to the meaning of what is more a short film more than just a video clip. The most likely, and one that is corroborated by Boris himself in his official blog, is that it is a dramatic anti-abortion message (the prison belongs to an imaginary Department of Control - implying 'birth control') for religious and moral reasons: the official/prostitute played by Lena represents an authority whose power is invested by the murkier vices of society, rather than the desire for justice, while the varied characters who are amused by the execution (businessmen, socialites, young orientals, a policeman, a Catholic priest, a black African) symbolise a falsely-moralistic and totally insensitive society that requires defenceless young women like Julia to execute the babies they are carrying.

Lena and Julia live up totally to the parts they're given. Julia looks proud and contemptuous - the way she can also be in real life - but at the same time resigned to her fate, whilst Lena is convincing as an authoritative and provocative troop commander. The setting is perfect, the drama of the lyrics and the addictive rhythm of the music come together perfectly, and the resulting video is a masterpiece in the history of music clips; it's hard to believe that it was shot in just one weekend, working from Saturday afternoon through till the early hours, and similar hours on the Sunday. Accounts from the set tell how Julia's ankles bears marks from walking more than a kilometre in real shackles, how Lena has a cold from the hours of filming during the chilly October nights barefoot and in skimpy clothing, and finally Troy, still in the uniform he was wearing as one of the guards in the firing squad, having fun backstage with his friends in the band (who can also be picked out in the video as members of the crowd cheering at the execution site).

A rumour circulates over the months that follow amongst t.A.T.u.'s fans that at first Lena had romantically refused to order any execution of her Julia, even a simulated one, but the rumour proves to be completely unfounded. Two years later the boots that Lena wore for the execution scene are auctioned on the official t.A.T.u.

website, along with the ripped fishnet stockings she was wearing in the early scenes; they fetch the incredible sums of $800 and $1,387 respectively.

The *Beliy Plaschik* video also represents the third and final part of t.A.T.u.'s 'murder trilogy'. For part one Julia and Lena together overthrow Vanja with the road train in *Nas Ne Dogonyat,* for part two Julia blows Lena up on the carousel in *30 minutes* and finally in this latest video Lena shoots Julia in front of the whole band.

The aim of the *Beliy Plaschik* video, the same as for other t.A.T.u. videos, is to shock and scandalise: for the first time in the final version of a video the girls appear partially (Julia) or fully (Lena) nude (for *Prostye Dvizheniya* Julia was topless but her breasts were not seen in the final version). Years later Katina recalls[186] having to overcome severe her aversion to filming the bedroom scene.

Two official versions of the video are distributed, the initial censored version for television broadcasting and a second version distributed widely across the internet months later; there are significant differences between them. The uncensored video is almost twice as long (and obviously contains a different arrangement of the song), with a long introduction lasting a little under a minute and during which there's a rapid succession of alternately static and moving images of scenes from later in the video, some of which do not actually appear in the official version (outdoor scenes where the characters are drinking, the control room etc.) In the video that follows there are shots where Julia bares her breasts in the shower, Lena takes off her bra and pants, the camera pans over Lena's naked body on the bed, Lena puts on her trousers and ties her tie, and so on. Another difference, obviously linked to the controversy stirred up by the *All About Us* video over the consumption of strong alcohol, is in the bottle that Julia is offered across the table: in the censored version it's red

---

[186] *"Лена Катина: 'В любовь с Волковой я не играла.Все было по-настоящему'", Moskovskiy Komsomolets,* 1 October 2011.

wine, while in the uncensored version it's a crystal decanter and after taking a sip Julia makes a face typical of someone tasting a highly potent spirit (in the behind-the-scenes shots the fake spirit is identified as tequila). The main difference is that the censored version doesn't contain scenes with the characters drinking and laughing as they watch the execution, a detail obviously deemed too challenging for general TV viewing.

Whilst they're waiting for the video to come out, Lena and Julia appear on the cover of the November issue of OK! Magazine Russia, which devotes a lengthy article to them, and they're inserted in the list of the one hundred sexiest women in Russia drawn up by Maxim magazine: Julia is in 15th place and Lena 53rd.

On November 29, the censored version of the *Beliy Plaschik* video is placed exclusively on MTV Russia's playlist for a fortnight and is an instant success. A few days later it is uploaded to Youtube by a few fans and immediately leaps to most-played video in Russia. In spite of the sensation that the shocking video causes, *Beliy Plaschik* doesn't have the hoped-for success as a single and is never a real hit: the times when t.A.T.u. songs were at the top of the charts are now definitively over, as Rensky writes in the forum blog in December:

> Many of you desire t.A.T.u. to get into tops by all means.. Have you thought this could cost your favorite group the loss of the face and the creative death? Neither t.A.T.u. did ever fit their art to Procrustes' bed of market's demands, nor they're gonna. (Insider user, 2007)[187]

---

[187] Tatu.ru official blog, post by *Insider*, 24 December 2007.

THE TWILIGHT OF T.A.T.U.

On 7th December the STS TV network devotes an episode of the program 'History In Details' to t.A.T.u. It shows an agitated Julia before the birth of her second child dealing with preparations for the baby's room in her villa on the outskirts of Moscow where she lives with Parviz. This is a different Julia from the one of a few years earlier who seems set on creating a proper family, as Lena confirms: 'Julia used to live only for the present, now she's thinking about the future too.' The TV cameras follow t.A.T.u. around the photo shoot they're doing for the Russian edition of men's magazine Maxim too: after nearly five years of the famous publication in which they were pictured in lingerie when they were eighteen, the wild-child girls are back bringing scandal to the December cover with a sexy picture of Lena posing with her arms around Julia and her baby bump. In the article inside Lena talks about the artistic future of t.A.T.u.:

> Sometimes you start thinking about a possible solo career, and Julia thinks about it more than I do. Personally, I might stop singing altogether if something happened to t.A.T.u. I'm a woman now, and I hope to be a mother someday and bring up my children. (Lena Katina, 2007)[188]

On 12th December news of the release of the maxi-single of *Beliy Plaschik* in February is announced on t.A.T.u.'s official website, and also that release of the album *Upravlenie Otbrosami,* which

---

[188] Alexey Karaulov, *"Праздник живота", Maxim Russia,* January 2008

the press had said was coming out on December 25, has been postponed to April 2008.

On Christmas Eve t.A.T.u. post a video greeting on My Space in which Julia and Lena apologise to their Russian fans for the delay in releasing the album (which they promise will be released in the spring) and announce that the new single (*Beliy Plaschik*) will be released in early 2008. Two days later Julia is at a party in Moscow with Parviz when she has to be rushed to hospital by ambulance[189]. The next morning, December 27, Julia gives birth to little Samir. It's not a real live recording of the birth as Julia had jokingly announced[190] it was to be some months earlier, but nevertheless Julia is filmed by Parviz with a videocamera on the bed in the clinic surrounded by all the medical equipment monitoring her, and she describes to her fans what she is feeling just before giving birth. The video is circulated on the internet the same day.

Julia and Lena take a month off in January 2008: just half a day is set aside for the dubbing of their few scenes in the film in the Moscow studios. Lena takes a short break in Cuba with her close friend Nastya whose wedding she was recently a witness for.

On 1st February MTV Ukraine shows the behind-the-scenes video of *Beliy Plaschik,* a full documentary that lasts about an hour which is then included on the DVD enclosed with selected versions of the maxi-single.

In mid-February the news (unofficial as yet) is released that a t.A.T.u. concert is to be held on 6th March at the Hub at UCSB (University of California, Santa Barbara) and the 800 seats will be available to students. The event is sponsored by the Russian students club at the prestigious university.

On February 20 Julia celebrates her 23rd birthday with Parviz, her family, the group's staff and of course Lena, who has recently

---

[189] "БЕРЕМЕННОЙ 'ТАТУ ШКЕ' вызвали 'скорую '", *Tvoi Den,* 25 December 2007.

[190] Mariya Remizova, "' ТАТУШКА ' Юля Волкова будет рожать в прямом эфире", *Komsomolskaya Pravda,* 18 October 2007

returned to Moscow from Cuba. Among the gifts she receives, as she tells in her online journal, are a jewellery box from Lena and 501 red roses from Parviz (as well as a Mercedes).

At the end of the month Julia and Lena leave separately for Los Angeles to shoot the video for *220* on 2nd March, which will be the second single from their next album. Two versions of the video are made (but this is only discovered some time later when a clip of the rejected version is tracked down on the internet by some fans), both directed by James Cox. It's a much simpler video than t.A.T.u.'s followers are accustomed to: in the rejected version Julia and Lena in transparent plastic coats through which their exquisite lingerie underneath can clearly be seen are singing in a room with mirrored walls, moving around amongst cables and hanging light bulbs that slowly brighten and dim. Only the beginning part of the video is found on the internet, which is probably just a demo.

The official video is filmed over a single, long day between 6.30am and midnight, in a purpose-built set inside a photographic studio in Santa Barbara, to the north of Los Angeles. The video is designed to be reminiscent of the predecessors of music videos from the 50s: the band in the background are almost unrecognisable in dark suits and with brilliantined hair, Lena and Julia in the foreground are dressed in corsets, stockings, gloves and hats, singing into vintage microphones. The girls perform a few dance steps in sync (which they have practised for three days with choreographer Sho-tyme), but overall the video is fairly static and certainly the least 'tatuistic' of all their videos (along with *Gomenasai* perhaps). Julia is the real star of the video (she has almost all the close-ups) and of the song which was written by Valery Polienko, singing all the verses while Lena joins in just for the chorus.

On March 5, the official website announces that the *Beliy Plaschik* maxi-single will be released at the end of the month as a CD and

DVD called *Hyperion Plate*, after the installation where the video was filmed. Inside the pack fans find also a voucher worth 50 rubles against the next album, the CD with *Beliy Plaschik,* the new track *220* and five remixed versions from the first CD, and on the DVD both the original censored and full-length versions of the video, the behind-the-scenes video, other bonus tracks and some photos. The first thousand packs are numbered and autographed by Julia and Lena (a video of the girls shot whilst they're signing the final copies is also circulated on the internet). This date too - as usual - is put off, and the maxi-single only becomes available in May.

On the evening of March 6 t.A.T.u. perform what is the first real concert in the United States for the eight hundred students gathered inside the Hub at UCSB (tickets are sold out quickly). The programme includes almost all the songs from the *Dangerous & Moving Tour* with the addition of *White Robe* - the English version of *Beliy Plaschik* - performed for the very first time. In an interview[191] held immediately after the performance with the college newsletter, Julia and Lena confess that they were a little nervous but full of energy when they went on stage; they then say that they have no more concerts planned in the US for the moment because they're very busy in Europe, but hope to be in San Francisco in June. In spite of these good intentions, Julia and Lena never return to perform as a duo in the United States.

On 25th March they have a concert scheduled at the Ice Arena in Minsk, Belarus, but a week before the event the organisers announce that it is postponed to 2nd May, due to problems beyond the control of t.A.T.u.

Julia and Lena take advantage of the change of date (the concert is later cancelled altogether) to rehearse with the band for a forthcoming concert in Dubai. On the 26th the whole group arrives in UAE ready for the concert and Julia and Lena give an interview

---

[191] *"t.A.T.u. Reflects on UCSB Concert, Future Plans", Daily Nexus,* 10 March 2008.

to the local newspaper Business 24-7 in which they confirm that the Russian version of the new album is almost ready (the delay being not in the distribution of the record, but in its production) and the CD should be out in late spring, whilst the English version is still far from ready and they're talking about autumn. In answer to a direct question Lena then says that t.A.T.u. at the moment are not signed to any record label and are still looking for a suitable one.

Concerning the group's scandalous image Lena once again confirms that it' s all in the past:

> Now we're both 23 years old we can't do that anymore. We're grown up, and our fans have grown up. (Lena Katina, 2008)[192]

In Dubai, t.A.T.u. go on stage dressed casually (Julia is wearing a Linus tee-shirt and miniskirt, Lena a black vest and jeans) and perform the same programme they did in California, with some slight changes in the order of the songs. There's a large audience at Media City and they're quite responsive, but the girls are in the wrong key a few times at the beginning, their performance is less than impressive and it doesn't go down as well as usual. A few months later in a radio interview[193] Julia and Lena explain that they'd had a few problems which had led to lengthy discussions with the local organisers up until shortly before the concert, so they were emotionally drained by the time they went on stage.

> The set-backs we had in Dubai were mainly technical, there was no particular problem, but the fact is that the concert didn't go as well as it should have. (Sven Martin, 2012)

---

[192] Rachel McArthur, 'All grown up and ready to return," Business24-7, 28 March 2008.

[193] 7 премьеры, 7 Radio Moscow, 23 October 2008.

A user calling himself Insider has been posting on the blog on t.A.T.u.'s official website for almost a year. His posts start in June 2007 with some revelations about t.A.T.u.'s past and continue in the following months with comments and insinuations in response to other users, as well as hints about the group's projects and 'behind the scenes' activities. Officially, Insider is a username under which any member of the t.A.T.u. staff including the girls can post from time to time. In fact, Insider is always used by the boss Boris Rensky, writing under a pseudonym so that he can freely express his own opinions about people who oppose the group, from the media to show business personalities.

But getting back to the concert in Dubai, a number of criticisms of Lena and Julia's performance appear on the forum immediately after the show, starting with the delay at the start (not uncommon for a t.A.T.u. concert), the way the girls looked, and finally the lack of enthusiasm they showed on stage. Some time later a comment by Insider endorses the criticism and places responsibility for what happened entirely on Julia and Lena:

> I agree. There was zero energy, their eyes were blank, their clothes looked like they'd just walked up on stage randomly on their way back from the corner shop. It's all true. The girls were probably exhausted, but that's no excuse: a professional must always, under all circumstances, give a top notch performance even if they're close to death or playing to an empty room. (Insider user, 2008)[194]

Insider concludes by announcing that he'll start work immediately on correcting the errors and improving the show by reviewing the show's dramatic content, the programme and anything else that might make t.A.T.u. concerts unforgettable.

---

[194] Tatu.ru official blog, post by *Insider*, 16 April 2008.

This is an unprecedented public attack by the girls' operational management (whether it's Rensky in person or one of his close associates makes no difference), and it can't fail to provoke a reaction. It's Lena who reciprocates in her online journal on April 25 in an unusually decisive manner: she says she is saddened by how things went in Dubai, but at the same time rejects accusations of a lack of emotional engagement:

> No matter how crazy or not-so-crazy we are on stage, we never perform without emotions. Do you really think we have no idea about what we sing?!... I'm shocked. (Lena Katina, 2008)

At the same time, Lena says she's ready to follow Insider's directions because a professional should always give '200%' and announces that she'll soon be moving to Los Angeles for two months with Julia to work on improving the show. But there will be no time for improvements or rebuilding: this is one of the last storms that attack the old 'battleship Таtу' while it's still afloat.

> A lot of people think artists should be like robots, but we're not robots, we're human beings. (Lena Katina, 2013)

Meanwhile, as mentioned above, the concert in Minsk is officially cancelled over problems that have come up with the local organisers, and t.A.T.u.'s management on the official website infer that the authorities are stonewalling the group.

On April 25 (before Lena posts the famous speech on her online journal) the girls are in the studio for the radio premiere of *220* as part of the Russkoye Radio morning show. The track stays exclusively on the Moscow station's playlist for a week, and the video is scheduled to debut at the beginning of June, but once again the schedule is not adhered to.

On 3rd May t.A.T.u. perform again, but only as part of a festival at Poklonnaya Gora, within the Victory Park area of Moscow. They sing the two singles from the new album live, without the band: *Beliy Plaschik* and then *220* after changing on stage to the delight of the audience.

Two days later, Julia and Lena fly to Sharm el-Sheikh for a concert that was planned a year ago to be held in the marketplace. Precise agreements are in place between the Egyptian music TV channel and the girls, to prevent them from hugging and kissing during the show which is being pre-recorded before broadcasting, but all efforts are in vain: Julia appears on stage first in a semi-transparent dress and then corset and knickers, and the broadcasting bosses decide not to show it.

On May 8 a new t.A.T.u. concert is announced in the United States, which will take place on June 6 at the Avalon Club in Santa Clara, California, and two days later t.A.T.u. perform at the Body and Soul gay club in Moscow, once again without the band.

Julia and Lena go to Cannes for a few days on May 15 for the premiere of the film *You and I* as part of the hors concours film festival.

The international press are treating t.A.T.u. as the real stars of the film, overlooking Mischa Barton, who decides to boycott the official screening even though she's in Cannes. Julia and Lena also have the opportunity to perform live with the whole band in one of the exhibition halls built for the event along the Croisette, and they perform *220* and *Beliy Plaschi*k as well as the soundtrack to the film, *You and I.*

From Cannes, Julia and Lena fly without the band to Verona, for their first (and only) proper concert in Italy. The venue is Club Skylight, a nightclub in St. Boniface of moderate capacity where t.A.T.u. play a late night programme (starting at around 2am) of just ten songs.

When t.A.T.u. are back in Russia their management announces the postponement of a concert scheduled for May 29 in Osnabruck, Germany to the new date of October 12.

There's a concert in St. Petersburg on 21st May preceded by an autograph session at the Soyouz shopping centre for the release of the *Hyperion Plate* maxi-single of *Beliy Plaschik*. The concert is supposed to begin around 9pm at Tiffany's Cafe but - as the online magazine Paparazzi.ru reports the following day[195] - Julia complains of having such severe dizzy spells just a few minutes before that the organisers have to call an ambulance. The paramedics give Julia first aid and decide to transfer her to a nearby hotel so that treatment can be administered in calmer surroundings, and Lena offers to hold the concert alone so as not to disappoint the hundreds of fans who have travelled to St. Petersburg from other countries specially for the concert. The concert starts more than two hours late and Lena delivers the performance reasonably well under the circumstances (apart from getting some of Julia's lyrics wrong), and includes almost the entire programme of songs that they'd planned except for *Nas Ne Dogonyat*, *Ne Zhalej* and *220* (which Julia usually sings almost solo). During the performance Lena apologises to the audience for her mistakes, saying that a solo career obviously doesn't suit her and that she can't sing alone. Her words turn out to be anything but prophetic.

Julia soon recovers and returns to Moscow with Julia the next day, with no ill effects.

On June 2, the official website announces the premiere of the *220* video, set for the night between the 4th and 5th of the month on Youtube. The group's management has decided to use this network after refusals by MUZ TV and MTV Russia to put the new video on their playlists. The two Russian music stations, which have always endorsed pop music videos, have incredibly rejected

---

[195] *t.A.T.и. спешат успокоить фанатов: Юле уже лучше*, Paparazzi.ru. 23 May 2008.

t.A.T.u.'s latest video which is less offensive and more truly pop-oriented, after showing all their other videos from *Ya Soshla S Uma* right through to the latest one, *Beliy Plaschik*, which were way more controversial. The official excuse, as Lena tells a few months later in Time Out magazine[196], is that the video is boring and - inexplicably - not suitable for their playlists. But it can't be as simple as that: there must be something else behind the refusal, and Insider speculates what it is on the blog, claiming that 'some of the music broadcasting monopolies are punishing t.A.T.u. for their independence' but admitting that they have no evidence to that effect and not wanting to insinuate that there's any conspiracy. The fact is that other music channels in Poland, Ukraine, Bulgaria and Greece decide to broadcast *220* straight away, and after a few weeks MTV Russia also joins them, but not MUZ TV.

The big US concert is planned for 6th June, but only two days before this a statement confirming that Julia is sick and has not been able to make the flight to Los Angeles appears on the official website, signed by Boris Rensky in person - an unusual occurrence. So the concert is cancelled at only two days' notice, and Rensky is asking for support for Julia at this difficult time. Fans take these words from the boss very seriously and are worried; best wishes for Julia's speedy recovery flood onto the various forums.

The reality, or rather the truth, of what Rensky claims, since Julia has never confirmed nor denied it, is very different according to what the boss himself reveals on Lena's official VK social network page[197] in July 2012, answering questions from fans :

> Julia simply refused to fly from Moscow to the Los Angeles, saying that she now had a fear of planes. I don't want to go into a

---

[196] Georgy Birger, *"t.A.T.и.: "Там же одни проститутки"*, *Time Out Magazine Russia*, no.34, 1-7 September 2008.

[197] *Интервью с Борисом Ренским*, VK Lena Katina official page vk.com/lenakatinaofficial, July 4, 2012.

description of the real reasons for Yulia's behavior, but for all of us internally, believe me, they were obvious and did not look in any way excusable. The concert was cancelled, we paid a huge fine, were ashamed and got onto the blacklist of people with which not to do business. And Yulia, after several days, flew to take a vacation. Her fear of flying disappeared without a trace.
(Boris Rensky, 2012)

Rensky goes on to say that he gave Julia a clear ultimatum in June 2008, 'If you do anything like that again, I'm leaving t.A.T.u.'
Whether or not things went exactly as the boss describes is not known, but the fact is that after this incident t.A.T.u. never do another real concert with the band (even the one in Osnabruck in October is finally cancelled), live performances are first of all restricted to just clubs, private parties and TV programmes, and then suspended altogether in 2009. Like the *Aurora* in St. Petersburg in 1944, after a long, hard battle against the flak 'battleship Тату' has now sunk: the crew is still officially together but drifting in a lifeboat that's too small to cope with the conditions and cannot stay afloat much longer.
The month of June ends without further excitement: the girls appear on the cover of Neon in which they talk about their latest single, and Lena updates her online journal to reassure fans about Julia's health; fans who are by now impatient with continual postponements of the release of the album and uncertainty about when the film will come out. At least they can be confident about Julia's condition, as she appears in excellent health accompanied by Parviz with Lena and her fiancé at the wedding of *You and I* producer Sergey Konov to actress Ekaterina Rednikova on 5th July.
On July 25 t.A.T.u. perform at a private party for a bank holding company at the Neskuchy Gardens in Moscow. Photographers from online magazine Paparazzi.ru get a glimpse[198] of an

---

[198] *ТАТУ В НЕСКУЧНОМ САДУ*, Paparazzi.ru, 28 July 2008.

unidentified CD on Parviz's dashboard, with a post-it stuck to it saying, 'Snegopady third single.' This is the first hint of the title of t.A.T.u.'s latest (and last, as it later turns out) single.

A few days later news is broadcast over the internet that the new album *Upravlenie*, the release date for which has been repeatedly set and then postponed, will finally be released on 2nd September. On 13th August there's more news, about the *220* single this time; it's reached no.1 in the MTV Russia chart and no.3 in the Channel 1 Russia chart.

In mid-August it's also reported that Julia and Lena have done a photo shoot for fashion designer Marc Jacobs as an endorsement of his autumn-winter collection.

(UN) HAPPY SMILES

By the first week of September there's still no trace of the album, but an extensive interview with Julia and Lena is published in the weekly Time Out magazine, in which they refer to the new album for the first time as *Vesyolye Ulybki* (*Happy Smiles*) rather than *Upravlenie Otbrosami* (*Waste Management*). A few days later the album is officially announced and in the press release[199] the group's managers explain the controversial reasons for the change of title:

> For almost a year a working title of the album was "Upravleniye Otbrosami" / "Waste Management". But a month before the release - for the sake of ironic smile of those, who understand – the title changed. The essence, however, remained. (Press-kits, 2008)

There are many interpretations of this cryptic statement and the change of name for the album. First interpretations would lead us to believe that this is the latest episode of 'tatuism' - their opposition and especially that of their managers to show business and its rules; another mocking gesture to critics and conformists who'd already celebrated t.A.T.u.'s premature demise. But after four years, and after Rensky's public outburst where he threatened to leave t.A.T.u., they may now have a different outlook.

---

[199] *Happy Smiles* press release T.A. Music.

It may be apt to consider what Rensky wrote on the blog under the title 'Happy Smiles' in an Insider post dated 11 September 2008[200]; in it he tells a story described as though it's a dream, in which he goes on a journey into space with two other astronauts; he tells of their beaming smiles for the photographers as they set off and the incredible emotion they experience during the voyage. When it's time for the return journey something goes wrong, there's noise and smoke in the capsule and they're only kept alive by their space suits and helmets which are still full of oxygen. 'Brace yourselves girls, we're plummeting out of control, it's going to be a hard landing!' But the parachute opens, the capsule slows down and they touch down gently. The crew open the door and step out, the horizon is a reddish colour, strange and empty. Their space boots touch sand...but there's not supposed to be sand at the landing site. The commander shouts 'Don't open your helmets! We're not on earth!' This is the epilogue that follows, word for word:

> People use to live through emotions, this-minute's emotions. And good for them. A happy smile would not be always possible if we knew our future. God saved us from this knowledge... (user Insider, 2008)

The allegory was covert at the time but now seems clear: the ship has a crew of three, the commander says 'brace yourselves, girls'... Boris couldn't be more explicit here: the message is not meant for fans or critics but for Lena and especially Julia; the photographers at the start, the joy of success, the happy smiles when things are going well. But the future is not always rosy: those who just live in the present only smile because they don't know what the future holds for them.

---

[200] Tatu.ru official blog, post by *Insider*, 11 September 2008.

> At the time the album title was changed to Happy Smiles Boris
> had not yet decided to put an end to t.A.T.u., but we were all
> truly exhausted and didn't know which way to go. (Lena Katina,
> 2013)

But for the moment life goes on: on 8th September a large group of fans is invited to attend a preview of the film *You and I* to gauge public perception of it; on this occasion however, it is announced that the film will not be released in cinemas before 2009.

On September 11, the day before the Bacardi B-Live music event, t.A.T.u. are expected at NRJ Energy Radio in Moscow to appear on the morning show. Lena turns up unexpectedly alone and gives no official reason for Julia's non-attendance.

The following day the single *You and I* debuts exclusively on the LoveRadio playlist. In the evening, t.A.T.u. perform with the band at the Bacardi B-Live festival in Moscow where they play thirteen tracks including *220*, *Vremya Luni*, *Zhaley* and *You and I* from the new album; Julia notices Ivan Shapovalov amongst the audience and nods a greeting to him.

On September 24 the Russia.ru station[201] starts broadcasting a mini reality series on t.A.T.u. over the web, entitled t.A.T.u. Life. The TV cameras follow Julia and Lena for a few months and broadcasting starts with images of them backstage at Bacardi B: Julia arriving late as usual (this time she blames car problems), a ritual rather than warm greeting for Lena who is waiting outside the venue, and their arrival on stage. Compared to previous reality shows filmed years before, it cannot go unnoticed in t.A.T.u. Life that the girls, now adults, are less engaged and almost totally independent of each other.

In early October t.A.T.u. are in Warsaw to receive the special prize at the VIVA Comet Awards, where they are headlining. Julia and Lena give interviews on radio and TV and meet their fans: their

---

[201] *t.A.T.u. Life*, Russia.ru TV Ep.1.

popularity in Poland is still very high and there is enormous anticipation for their live TV performance. Polish television has specifically requested that the original version of *Ya Soshla S Uma* is included in the programme as it is more popular in Poland than the English version, but during rehearsals Julia and Lena discover that the arrangement they've brought with them has their voices in the forefront with Julia 'screeching' in the refrain and in the counter melody, which is impossible for her to produce now. Julia is very upset: it's unthinkable to sing three quarters of the song with the voices of two 23-year-olds and lip-sync the rest of it with teenager voices, especially in front of an audience. Despite the insistence of the Polish TV Julia and Lena perform *All The Things She Said* in English (in addition to *White Robe, 200* and the new songs) to the enthusiastic appreciation of the audience, but the circumstances are emblematic of the those long ago days of 2000, and how far and how haphazardly t.A.T.u. have now moved on from those little girls who touched the hearts of so many young people eight years ago. At the end of their performance Julia and Lena throw the trophy they've just received smilingly into the audience.

After celebrating Lena's 24th birthday in Poland on October 4 (her present from her boyfriend is a trip in a hot air balloon), t.A.T.u. are in Donetsk in Ukraine on the 12th for the Ukrainian European Television Music Awards where they perform *You and I.*

The new album *Vesyolye Ulybki* is released on 21st October, and for the occasion Julia and Lena are at the Soyuz megastore in Moscow to meet fans and autograph posters and CDs.

Interviewed by Russia.ru for the reality show t.A.T.u. Life, young people at the entrance are excited to finally be able to buy a new album after three years of waiting, and also to have their photographs taken with their idols; the girls meet them wearing tee-shirts made by fans of the official forum with all their names printed on them.

Within two weeks *Vesyolye Ulybki* becomes the biggest selling album in Soyuz music stores, which is the only outlet where the CD is available for the moment.

On November 28 t.A.T.u. are the headline guests at the MTV Russian Music Awards in Moscow. Julia and Lena ride onto the red carpet on two Kawasaki motorcycles, wearing leather jackets and helmets. It was the middle of winter, but the girls had been learning how to ride for a few days with the help of professional instructors for their unprecedented entry to the RMA, channelling their new video *Snegopady*. Shortly after t.A.T.u. are called up on stage to receive the award for MTV Legend: as part of his introduction the presenter says, 'their arrival has changed the definition of Russia, which now reads: Red Square, bears, caviar, t.A.T.u.'

Despite the riding lessons and the reference made at RMA, Julia and Lena never actually appear on any motorcycles in the final version of the *Snegopady* video as the entire second part is generated by computer. After a string of t.A.T.u. videos produced in the United States, this latest one is directed by Boris Rensky and is filmed, like their very first one was, in Russia. The video opens with the last fifteen seconds of *220* and follows on from it, with Julia going down to the dressing rooms after the performance to change her clothes. Lena is already there and watches her go past. The shot of them putting on canvas trainers and leather jackets (the same ones they wore at the RMA) switches by computer graphics to outside where the girls, each riding her own motorcycle, engage in a reckless chase (preceded by a warning for young people not to copy them) that ends dramatically with the two riders deliberately crashing into one other. Whether this ending was intended as a metaphor for the demise of the group, which was already on the cards, or whether it's a coincidental portent, is unclear.

On November 29 t.A.T.u. are to take part in the Children's New Wave youth singing competition as guests and judges. The

Russia.ru TV cameras are there at the rehearsals and immortalise the row between the girls (backed by Boris) and the programme director, who wants to have t.A.T.u. singing on stage alone, whilst Julia and Lena insist on having the children around them. The dispute is resolved in Julia and Lena's favour - the director is overruled - they direct their own performance with the help of Boris and sing *Ne Zhaley* with the children.

On 10th December the official website announces that t.A.T.u. will be the main stars at the B1 Maximun Club in Moscow for MTV's New Year Party. The whole band will be there, as confirmed by Troy MacCubbin in his blog on the 12th, when he says he's about to leave for Moscow for two t.A.T.u. concerts taking place within two weeks. A few hours before his departure however, he receives a countermand from Moscow: all December performances are cancelled because Julia is ill. The announcement is only made at 7.45 on December 16 on the group's Facebook page; for the record, on the afternoon of that day Julia was photographed looking in good health with Parviz and Vika at the Neposedi party.

This is the point when the ultimatum that Boris made in June is finally brought to bear; as he himself recalls in 2012, the MTV Party episode is almost a repeat of what happened at the concert in the United States; Julia seems to have ignored the warning and the result of this will soon be felt.

In the meantime Julia and Lena perform without the band on 26 December at a private party at the Dorffman restaurant and karaoke bar in Moscow.

The darkness that is starting the descend around t.A.T.u.'s future is not apparent in the new year greetings video that Julia and Lena put out on the internet: their 'happy smiles' are as cheerful as ever.

THE END OF THE T.A.T.U. PROJECT

The year 2009 opens with the good news that the *220* video is voted by the public as MTV Russia's Video of the Year; although it is certainly not the most memorable of t.A.T.u.'s videos the firepower of their fans worldwide (voting took place over the internet in the last 10 days of December) easily beat the local competition.

t.A.T.u. have no official engagements in January: no performances, no photo shoots, nothing at all. Julia and Lena are only photographed together at the premiere of the film Valkyrie. Julia is also photographed at the premiere of another film, Australia, on February 10, in the company of Parviz and Alexey Mitrofanov. In the following few days Julia goes to Los Angeles where she spends her 24th birthday. In this period Julia meets one of t.A.T.u.'s fans, an avid contributor to the forum on the official Tatu.ru website (going by the name *yulialena21*) and confides to her that she wants to start a solo career in the United States, but without wishing to leave t.A.T.u.

The confidence is kept secret, but when an article in the online magazine Paparazzi.ru in mid-March[202] reports a rumour (from another source), according to which Julia is about to leave t.A.T.u. and has already recorded two duets with Lady Gaga, the girl decides to disclose it to reassure fans about the future of the group. But by now the panic has spread and news of Julia's farewell to t.A.T.u. reverberates across all the online forums and blogs. The

---

[202] *ВОЛКОВА ПРОМЕНЯЛА ТАТУ НА LADY GAGA,* Paparazzi.ru, 19 March 2009 .

same site Paparazzi.ru[203], an hour after releasing the first report on 19th March, tries to acquire some kind of direct confirmation and finally manages to contact Volkova, who denies that she's had any kind of collaboration with Lady Gaga and states that she hasn't the least intention of terminating the partnership with Lena, even to follow a solo career.

What actually happened leading up to this only becomes clear three years later when Boris Rensky recalls:

> One day in the beginning of 2009 I asked Lena and Yulia to come to the office. I officially announced to the girls, that my activity in t.A.T.u. was over, that I no longer wish to have any professional ties with Yulia. I offered Lena to work with me on her solo project and she agreed. Everything was done eye to eye without any plots or separate negotiations. This is how t.A.T.u. closed and Lena Katina's project opened. (Boris Rensky, 2012)[204]

So the t.A.T.u. project ends on a cold winter's day in Moscow exactly ten years after it began: without Rensky there's no money, no staff, and no management. There would only be, in effect, Julia Volkova and Lena Katina, but their relationship is no longer what it used to be: they're two close-knit professional colleagues who know each other well, they're no longer two sisters united by an unbreakable bond. We don't know and probably never will, whether in that office in Moscow whilst Boris was passing his final judgement on t.A.T.u., Julia and Lena exchanged a look, and whether one of them was waiting for the other - in vain - to reach out and give her hand an encouraging squeeze as they had done a hundred times in the past on stage. Their hands do not touch,

---

[203] *Юля Волкова не оставит t.A.T.u.* Paparazzi.ru, 19 March 2009, 21:12.

[204] *Интервью с Борисом Ренским,* VK Lena Katina official page vk.com/lenakatinaofficial, 4 July 2012.

neither of them feels compelled to propose that they continue on their own, this time really on their own, not like at the time of the breakup from Shapovalov when they were left with Boris. Deep down it's what they'd both been expecting for some time, probably for years: it was logical that sooner or later - as they became adults - they would each want to go their own way.

But in the period leading up to spring 2009 there are still many things to be taken forward; investments already made that have to be recouped and important agreements to be honoured. So it's too early to reveal that t.A.T.u. no longer exist, so Boris decides to put an end to the rumours already going round, which are only partly true.

On March 21, Insider writes a piece on the blog under the title t.A.T.u. forever[205]:

> Last December a "staff meeting" attended by Yulia, Lena and Boris took place. Parties had unanimously decided to cease the "operation of t.A.T.u. in full-time mode". This decision was not spontaneous, it was long-grown. [...]we will close all our "open items", i.e. we'll release the third video as it was promised, at the end of March - beginning of April, girls will do their part in promo campaign for "You and I" movie, which is being late on schedule due to circumstances beyond our command, but which is to be released surely. We'll also release a special long-play edition of "HS", with runtime more than an hour [...] Works on the show were suspended last June, and are not being planned. No public concerts are being planned, except some special events like *Bacardi*. (user Insider, 2009)

The statement goes on to specify that Julia will undertake a solo career completely independent of the t.A.T.u. staff who will be

---

[205] Tatu.ru official blog, post by *Insider*, 21 March 2009.

170

working with Lena to support the release of her first album between late 2009 and 2010.

Ultimately, what Boris said in the statement he made as Insider was the truth: this is in fact the declaration of liquidation, and they're only continuing as a group in order to carry out existing commitments, in the same way that a government does when it resigns. Only the most optimistic of fans can now believe there's any hope of a future for t.A.T.u. and that the story is not yet ended, despite the fact that Julia and Lena are already starting to work separately from each other.

In the afternoon of the same day that the statement is released, Julia meets her fans in Moscow and when asked about the future she explains that she and Lena are still friends, that she already has some demos of songs as a soloist, and goes on to compare the future of t.A.T.u. with that of the Black Eyed Peas (where the singer Fergie is pursuing a solo career alongside her work with the band).

The week after Julia repeats the comparison with Fergie in an interview with Moskovsky Komsomolets[206] and Lena adds, 'We still have to get used to the new situation ourselves, where it's not just t.A.T.u. any more, it's also Julia and I as two distinct artists.'

At the end of March Julia is photographed in two everyday situations without Lena.

At the beginning of April a trailer for the new video *Snegopady* is released. The introduction has a disturbing undertone and ends dramatically: '...they knocked at your heart, but they weren't allowed in; now all that remains is brutal revenge for your insensitivity...or death.' With the explosion at the end it's only too clear that this is a metaphor for the destiny of the group.

On 14th April Lena meets her fans in Moscow and confesses to them that she's quite anxious about starting a solo career as she's not had enough experience of performing alone (we know that it's

---

[206] *"Полураспад на поп-половинки"*, Moskovskiy Komsomolets, 27 March 2009.

in Lena's nature to be resistant to radical changes in her life). During the meeting with fans Lena receives a phone call in which Julia announces that the recording of *Sparks* (the English version of *220*) has been postponed.

The *Snegopady* video is played for the first time on the night of April 17 as part of the Newsblock feature on MTV Russia, and a few hours later two versions of it are uploaded to the internet: the TV version and a special version called '*heart attack*' with audio effects but no music.

On 19th April t.A.T.u. are due to perform at the State Kremlin Palace in Moscow as part of the 18th anniversary celebrations for Neposedi, as announced on the school's official website. But Lena is not there; she's in Los Angeles rehearsing with the band as a soloist. This is the first official occasion following their widely-known declaration a month ago on which it is made abundantly clear that the girls' professional lives no longer revolve around t.A.T.u. Julia appears at the show with former SMASH! member Sergey Lazarev, who also started out at Neposedi like Julia and Lena, and sings *Nas Ne Dogonyat* with help from the children and from Lazarev. This is the first time that Julia has ever sung a t.A.T.u. song on any official occasion without Lena at her side.

Two days later Julia gives an interview on Russian TV station HTB[207] where she reiterates how things stand: relations with Lena are excellent, each of them is concerned with her own solo career, the group has not been dissolved but has slowed things down.

On the other side of the globe Lena is still working with the band in Los Angeles, as Troy confirms on Twitter, but she also finds time to undergo laser eye surgery to correct her short-sightedness. The operation, which is carried out in an outpatient clinic at Stanford University, is recorded in detail by Russia.ru TV cameras: Lena appears cheerful but rather worried, as she confirms a few days later in her online journal.

---

[207] HTB News, 21 April 2004.

Lena returns to Moscow at the beginning of May; she and Julia are guests at the Eurovision Song Contest which is being held in the Russian capital this year. At the opening ceremony on the 10th they perform, lip-synching, to *Ne Ver, Ne Boysia*. Images of their 2003 performance scroll past on a megascreen beside the stage, and Lena and Julia look at each other and smile; they even hug, but in a rather theatrical way. At the semi-finals two days later t.A.T.u. give a memorable performance of *Not Gonna Get Us* not because of their singing (the whole song is lip-synched) but because the whole of the Red Army choir is on stage with them (they also lip-synch), as well as a vast array of dancers and even a pink tank and a blue MiG jet fighter, both made out of papier maché. The crowd goes into raptures, but there's not a lot left to see of t.A.T.u. on stage: Julia with bare legs, wearing high heels and a long ponytail looks more like a modern bond-girl than the saucy brunette she used to be, Lena appearing with her hair in pigtails which she has never done before, wearing a black kimono and intense make-up and looking like a young mother playing the little girl. t.A.T.u. are still very popular at home, and two autograph sessions are organised by the Eurovision sponsors in two supermarkets for the 13th and 16th of that month.

Around this time an edition of OK Magazine[208] is on the newsstands which, as well as having a new photo of the two girls together on the cover, contains an article on t.A.T.u. in which the girls look back over their ten years together:

> Everything that's happened to us in the last ten years has been extremely positive. I remember some terribly stressful times when we had three public appearances in the same day, and we didn't even have time for a wash or get something to eat before it was time to board another plane; we were totally exhausted. But

---

[208] Sergey Anisimov, "t.A.T.u.: 'Мы и сейчас иногда целуемся'", OK! Magazine Russia, no.20 (133) 2009.

it's nice looking back at those times now, and even if I could go back and change them, I wouldn't change anything, not one iota. (Lena Katina, 2009)

On May 23 there's an extraordinary sketch on NTV Channel's Russian Sensation programme that depicts Julia and Lena as apprentice road maintenance workers on the streets of Moscow, where the girls appear happy and smiling.

31st May is the tenth anniversary of t.A.T.u., and for the occasion MTV Russia broadcast a long interview with Julia and Lena the day before. It's particularly significant that an interview to celebrate the duo is conducted separately with each girl, whose professional lives are now totally separate from each other. But it's probably because of this very circumstance that Julia and Lena can now respond to questions about t.A.T.u. sincerely and personally, for the first time in the history of the band, as these words from Lena demonstrate:

> Julia and I are the opposite of each other. Julia always sees herself in the role of leader and has to have all attention focussed on her. And because I know this about her and I know what she's like, I always put myself in the background. (Lena Katina, 2009)[209]

In June t.A.T.u. appear on the cover of the monthly Bravo magazine. In the interview published inside[210] Julia takes the opportunity to complain about the way Russian show business operates compared to the serious business it is in the United States, and Lena backs her up by blaming the producers who, in her opinion, are only interested in turning a profit and don't reward creativity.

[209] *Newsblock*, MTV Russia, 30 May 2009.
[210] *"Это шоу-бизнес, детка!" BRAVO*, June 2009.

On the 5th of the month Julia and Lena arrive separately on the red carpet for the MUZ TV Awards, Julia accompanied by Parviz and Lena by her best friend Nastya. t.A.T.u., now broken and finished, sit amongst the audience and watch the performance by Serebro: the three-girl group launched to fame by Eurovision in 2007 and now well-known throughout Russia, and destined to take over from t.A.T.u. to become the second Russian group to break into the western market with their single *Mama Lover*.

At the beginning of July Lena is back in Los Angeles playing with the band; on the same day the English language version of the video for *Snegopady,* with the title *Snowfalls,* is uploaded to Youtube and after two days becomes the most requested video in the popular archive.

Lena writes her online journal in between sessions at Sven's recording studio; she appears calm and is enthusiastic about the work she's doing with the band; and she also mentions that she's bumped into Julia who's in Los Angeles to practice some new songs, and that she looked very well. Lena stays in Los Angeles until September, which is the month her official website as a solo artist is launched.

In October Lena returns to Moscow to celebrate her 25th birthday, meeting up with a group of fans first before going on to a restaurant with her close friends, including Boris and Julia, who sings for her.

In mid-October there are persistent rumours about the imminent release of the album *Waste Management,* confirmed a short time before by Lena in an interview with AIF magazine, which turn out to be not true. In the same interview Lena reveals her fears about the future of t.A.T.u.:

> Success doesn't last forever. At first I was desperate, I thought, 'Oh, no one needs us any more,' but fortunately this feeling soon passed when I realised we had a lot of fans all around the world

still listening to us. And waiting for something new from us. (Lena Katina, 2009)[211]

Around this time Lena and Julia also attend Russian Fashion Week in Moscow separately.

At the end of the month Coqueiro Verde Records, who are responsible for distributing the *Waste Management* CD, upload the English TV version of *Beliy Plaschik* (without the nude scenes) on Youtube. The only editing that's been done is to insert the lip movements for the song in English which was already filmed by Cox in 2007 along with the Russian version.

Meanwhile Lena has already returned to the U.S. and has her first experience of Halloween in America; she describes in her online journal on her personal website how amused she is to see what a peculiar way the Americans have of celebrating this annual event.

In November British digital TV company, BT Vision, announces a referendum amongst its users to choose the best pop video of the decade. *All The Things She Said* comes second[212] after Rihanna's *Umbrella*.

On November 18 it's announced on the official Tatu.ru website that Coquiero Verde Records will be distributing the album *Waste Management* in Brazil, Chile and Argentina on the 15th of the following month. The press release states that it will not be a mere transposition of the album *Vesyolye Ulybki* into English, but a non-stop LP in the style of Pink Floyd where each song blends into the next with an instrumental interlude (designed by Rensky and composed by Evgeniy Matveitsev); a unique idea in the music business. Boris later calls this version the *Transcendent Version* (because it is aimed at transcendental meditation) in one of his

---

[211] *"ТАТУШКА" Лена: У Ивана Шаповалова поехала крыша,* Newsmusic.ru, 30 September 2009.

[212] *"Rihanna's hit single 'Umbrella' has been voted the best pop video in the last 10 years",* Sawf News, 27 November 2009.

official blog posts as Insider[213]. The cover of *Waste Management* is totally different from the cover of the Russian album: not astronauts this time but Julia and Lena pictured in a filthy slum area wearing two dubious coats, evoking an image of poverty, even though they're wearing seductive lingerie under the coats. The picture is from a photo shoot in Moscow from May 2007[214]: the brainchild of Boris and filmed by Vladimir Byazrov, but the image has been graphically reworked and the girls' faces have been ripped. With regard to the title, the press release leaves no room for doubt:

> Actually the time has come to say it straight the "Happy Smiles" name was nothing more than a joke addressed to the t.A.T.u. fans' sense of humor. Really, this album was all about "Unhappily Unsmiling" in its very essence. To be more precise, it was *Waste Management*. (Press kits, 2009)

The South American record company is not able to meet the deadline of December 15 to commence distribution, and the version destined for the Russian market (which is identical except for the language used on the back of the insert) becomes available on the official website.

Shortly before the end of the year Julia and Lena prepare a video greeting for their fans as usual. In the video Lena mentions that 2009 was a difficult year for t.A.T.u. and says that she and Julia are still together, that everything is fine and that they'll be working together on something new and good for their fans in 2010. Despite the promises however, this video message will be the last thing they ever record together. Within the same few days Boris, as Insider, also greets bloggers for the last time.

---

[213] Tatu.ru official blog, post by *Insider*, 3 December 2009.
[214] *"t.A.T.u., рваные халаты и гамбургеры"*, *Hello! Magazine Russia*, 21 May 2007.

2010 opens with a big party for Russian fans organised through the official website Tatu.ru aboard a large barge on the Volga, where Julia and Lena appear smiling surrounded by fans, but demonstrate little enthusiastic affection for each other. Lena enjoys the evening very much and writes enthusiastically about the participants and organisers in her online journal.

Coquiero Verde continues to delay the release date of the album in South America, and February comes round: Julia's 25th birthday. Lena is noticeable by her absence from Julia's party at the Isterika club in Moscow; she tries in vain, as she reveals much later in an interview[215], to reach Julia by phone so she can at least wish her a happy birthday. A few days later Volkova announces the release of her first solo single in an interview on MUZ TV, set for the following summer.

Waste Management finally appears in record shops in South America on January 25, and Lena is interviewed by the Brazilian edition of Billboard[216] at the beginning of March about this latest album from t.A.T.u.

> Our new songs are more experimental, not our usual style, because our fans have grown up with us. Our image was crucial to start with, but now it's all about the music. (Lena Katina, 2010)

Two weeks later NTV broadcasts a documentary about Julia's solo career, where she talks for the first time about the genre of her first album which she calls 'sex-rock' and what t.A.T.u. will be involved with in the future:

---

[215] *"Лена Катина", Viva! Russia,* October 2011 .

[216] *"Imagem não é nada", Billboard Brazil,* March 2010.

t.A.T.u. will continue to exist, but we'll be like Pink Floyd, an album and a tour together every five years and then back to working as solo artists. (Julia Volkova, 2010)[217]

At the end of the month there's talk of a competition organised by Kroogi.com for the best remixed versions of the *Waste Management* track, where well-known and less well-known artists and DJs can submit their own arrangements in one of the five styles permitted: Downtempo, Deep House, Hip Hop, Psytrance and Dubstep. The best remixes will be included in an album destined to be the last official LP released by t.A.T.u.

On April 12 the video for *Sparks,* the English version of *220,* is broadcast for the first time on TV by MTV Brazil. Two days later Lena Katina's first solo concert is officially announced, to be held on 30th May at the historic Troubadour club in Los Angeles, which sells out.

The day before the concert Lena meets her fans, along with Troy and Sven, and answers many of their questions; regarding t.A.T.u. she says that the last album was completed at a particularly difficult time for them and that there are a lot of errors in it; errors that they've taken to heart. Lena also says that she's no longer recognised on the streets of Moscow: this revelation alone demonstrates how much the group's popularity has sunk in their own country, where only six years ago newspapers, TV and radio journalists couldn't get enough of them.

The next day Lena chooses seven t.A.T.u. songs as well as six new ones of her own (*World, IRS, Just a Day, Lost in Love, So Not Cool* and *Stay*) for her official debut as a soloist, and opens the concert with the Transformer remix of *Running Blind,* arranged by Sven and Julian Schramm who wrote the original version together. Everyone is nervous at the start: Lena starts singing with the microphone switched off and gets half way through the first song

---

[217] *Русская начинка,* NTV Russia, 20 March 2010.

without any amplification; she loses her headset in the middle of *All The Things She Said* and one of the two backing singers tries to help out by running over to her microphone. The harmonies are not always perfect in general, but the audience enthusiastically support Lena throughout the show by singing along to many of the songs and declaring the show to be a success. Several months later, in an interview with MK magazine[218], Lena confesses:

> At my debut as a solo singer at the [*author's note:* Troubadour] club my knees were like jelly, just like at t.A.T.u.'s first concert, but at the same time it was amazing and exciting to be there. (Lena Katina, 2011)

What's more, Lena had been through a period of depression in the months that followed the famous meeting in Moscow where the breakup of t.A.T.u. was decreed, brought on by her separation from Julia:

> I lost sleep, I wasn't eating, I just wore drab clothes and I was really sad. My mother advised me to get help from a specialist. [...] Over the several sessions I had with the psychologist he started to lead me out of this state of depression and away from my dependence on Julia. I was totally dependent on her, I couldn't imagine getting up on stage on my own. Julia was the leader on stage and in life, but slowly I gained confidence in myself. (Lena Katina, 2011)[219]

On 31st May Kroogi.com announces the fourteen winning remixes that will comprise, along with some bonus tracks, the forthcoming album *Waste Management Remixes.*

---

[218] *"Лена Катина: 'В любовь с Волковой я не играла.Все было по-настоящему'"*, Moskovskiy Komsomolets, 1 October 2011.
[219] *"Лена Катина"*, Viva! Russia, October 2011.

In June, OK! Magazine publishes a lengthy article and a photo shoot on Julia. Julia confirms rumours about her break-up with Parviz after living with him for three years, and talks about her solo career:

> I grew out of that little girl I used to be and realised I can do whatever I want. I work without a producer, I've put together a team and recorded some demos. I'll be going back to the US soon to record an album in the new 'sex-rock' genre that I've created. I've decided to go for the western market because show business just doesn't exist in my own country. [...] There's just a lot of hypocrisy and very little creativity. (Julia Volkova, 2010)[220]

On June 12 Lena performs at Pridefest in Milwaukee, Wisconsin: the historic American music event of the LGBT community. Lena's set, which closes the festival, is the same as she one she tried at the Troubadour club but with some slight changes, and Lena is far more confident than she was at her debut in Los Angeles; she interacts with the audience, sings *30 minutes* sitting confidently on the edge of the stage and ends with an overwhelming *Not Gonna Get Us*, jumping about amidst screaming from the audience like old times. One fan presents Lena and the other band members with handmade dolls of them all; Lena takes the one of Julia.

At the end of the month Julia, Lena and Sven meet up in Los Angeles. The photo that goes out across the various forums captures them smiling (Julia is holding the doll that Lena has just given her) and there's nothing to suggest that a few days on the most violent media clash will take place between the two (almost ex- at this point) t.A.T.u. girls.

On 17th July MTV Russia shows a vitriolic interview with Julia, recorded on 3rd June (so four days after Lena's debut at the

---

[220] *"Я Дам Фору ЛЮбому мужчине", OK! Russia Magazine,* 3 June 2010.

Troubadour) during the party to celebrate the return of Billboard magazine to Russia:

> There's one thing I don't understand: she introduces herself as Lena Katina, she creates a website as Lena Katina, so what the hell does she mean by singing t.A.T.u. songs like All the Things She Said and Not Gonna Get Us on 30th May at her 'first performance as Lena Katina?' [*author's note:* Julia gets confused and actually says 'June', but she's obviously referring to the end of the previous month]. Of course, she has the right, but it's stupid, absolutely stupid if she wants a solo career. [...] Her solo career will soon vanish. (Julia Volkova, 2010)[221]

The MTV interview causes an uproar amongst t.A.T.u. fans, who find themselves having to side with either Julia or Lena for the first time. Lena cannot abandon her fans, leaving them to the fratricidal struggle being played out on the forums, and decides to intervene by sending out a message of peace on her own video blog[222]:

> I saw Julia's interview and I was upset of course. But I want everyone to know that I have a completely opposite attitude towards the whole situation, Julia's project included. I believe that she's a very talented person and I sincerely hope that she will be successful in all the things she plans. (Lena Katina, 2010)

Lena's response is typically very peaceable and calm; and all the more understandable in the light of the events that led up to it: Lena performs solo at the Troubadour on May 30 and sings a number of t.A.T.u. songs; Julia is evidently put out by this and gives the interview with MTV four days later; even though the interview hasn't yet been broadcast the rumour quickly gets round

---

[221] *Hearing Test*, MTV Russia, 17 July 2010.
[222] Lena Katina official VEVO account, 20 July 2010.

and three weeks later Sven organises a meeting between Julia and Lena in Los Angeles, clearly with the intention of reconciling them. The photo of the three of them smiling shows that this objective was achieved. On July 12 Lena performs at Pridefest and again includes the t.A.T.u. songs in her set; the interview is broadcast on the 17th and the controversy erupts, but in the meantime the girls have already patched things up, allowing Lena to respond with extreme patience and understanding on her video blog.

In August, whilst MTV Brazil are showing the English-language video for *Snowfalls* for the first time, Julia announces a Glam Party to celebrate the launch of her own solo career at Club U2 in Moscow on 9th September. Julia turns up at the party with her new boyfriend Vadim.

Meanwhile the official tatu.ru website announces a new competition amongst fans, this time for the artwork for the cover of the new album of remixes containing the songs selected in the first competition.

During this time (the exact date is uncertain) Lena and Julia get together in Nuremberg, Germany, to pose for a fashion shoot. t.A.T.u. are the official endorsers of the 2011 collection of Humphrey's eyewear. The behind-the-scenes video shows them calm and happy like old times.

In late September Julia and Lena attend a party together organised by the music paper Billboard in Moscow, where they reveal themselves to be in tune with each other, seated for some length of time side by side, at least as far as appearances go. Lena also performs one of her new solo songs[223], *Lost In His Dance*, but after hearing it Julia doesn't scruple to disguise her doubts on MUZ TV, saying, 'I'm disappointed to be honest, I don't feel any energy... I find it really boring.'

---

[223] *ПАПАРАЦЦИ*, MUZ TV, 25 October 2010.

In November the winner of the competition to design of the cover of *Waste Management Remixes* is announced; the album will be distributed primarily online, but there will be a few physical copies (of which, however, there is no trace).

In January 2011 news gets round[224] that Volkova has acquired the majority of t.A.T.u. rights that were left with Boris Rensky. Rensky doesn't provide details of the sale, but confirms that Julia has a majority share of the t.A.T.u. brand.

Julia Volkova's website as a soloist also comes online in January. On the same day the official website of the film *You And I* in Russian, *Ty I Ya,* is launched; the film is due to be released in Russian cinemas on February 3.

At the film premiere in Moscow Lena and Julia are photographed and portrayed as the real stars of the event. Smiling in their evening gowns, the girls speak for the first into the MTV microphones of their experiences of the end of t.A.T.u.

> We stayed the same for 10 years, but now we've reached the end of the line: it's time to make a graceful exit. (Julia Volkova, 2011)[225]

The Moscow event is the last where Julia and Lena appear together officially as t.A.T.u.: they're just waiting for the album of remixes to come out before formally announcing their dissolution.

The film has no better luck: in the first two weeks of screening box office takings only amount[226] to the equivalent of $775,000, a real disaster for the producers considering that t.A.T.u. alone are owed $300,000 for their participation and the rights to use their song on the soundtrack. So even *You And I,* as expected, finds itself up against a vortex of problems, controversies, delays and legal

---

[224] *Юлия Волкова стала владелицей львиной доли бренда "ТАТУ"* Lifeshowbiz.ru, 28 January 2011.

[225] *Newsblock,* MTV Russia, 27 January 2011.

[226] *Суд да дело,* Lifeshowbiz.ru, 18 February 2011.

tangles, the same as everything else throughout the entire history of t.A.T.u., as the online publication Lifeshowbiz.ru reveals[227]. But time was the main cause of the failure of *You and I*, without a doubt: the idea of a movie (albeit a completely different film) had sparked as far back as 2003[228] when t.A.T.u. were at the peak of their popularity at home and abroad. But even *t.A.T.u. Come Back*, the title of which later became *You And I*, was announced[229] by Julia as far back as October 2006 when the girls were on tour in Russia and still filling the pages of weekly magazines and TV programmes. The last potential period when it could have been successful was spring 2008: immediately after Cannes, when relationships between Julia, Lena and Boris had not yet been completely eroded and a positive mutually-beneficial effect would have linked the film and t.A.T.u.'s third album, and may have warded off the dissolution of the group. But in 2011, with t.A.T.u. already broken up a year ago and their millions of fans dispersed, there was really no hope for the film either.

On February 20 Julia celebrates her 26th birthday and throws a party the following evening at a nightclub in Moscow to announce her new official website. Lena's absence from the party is noticeable, and irritably answering a question from one of the fans there, Julia says she didn't invite her (ex) partner because she was the only one she didn't receive good wishes from[230].

The album *Waste Management Remixes* is officially released to online stores on March 29, described in the press release as t.A.T.u.'s last record since Julia and Lena have already launched their solo careers at this time. The management just write a couple of words of adieu on the official Tatu.ru website:

---

[227] *Суд да дело*, Lifeshowbiz.ru, 18 February 2011.

[228] *ТАТУ СНИМУТСЯ В ЛЕСЬИЙСКОМ КИНО*, News.people, 25 November 2003.

[229] *News*, Tatysite.net, 27 October 2006.

[230] *Юля Волкова отпраздновала день рождения без Лены Катиной*, Life-star.ru, 22 February 2011.

Thanks to everyone who's been with us for almost eleven years.
Thank you to every single t.A.T.u. fan.

Six days later the leading American music paper Billboard.com officially announces the dissolution of the group with a short interview with Lena.

> People will remember us for great songs, being free, taking life as it is and not being afraid of anything. (Lena Katina, 2011)[231]

The story of t.A.T.u. officially ends on April 4, 2011 with the Billboard announcement (repeated in all the major music magazines around the world), but Lena celebrates the end of her long personal and professional history with Julia in a most original way a few months later, with the release of her first solo single. The song *Never Forget* (the original title was *Never Forget You)* - co-written by Lena - is in fact a touching farewell message:

> *We said that we were meant to be*
> *That we were each other's destiny*
> *And now we've faded away*
> ...
> *Our moments together*
> *I will keep forever*

And the message is rendered even more poignant by James Cox, enlisted once more by Lena and Boris to direct what may be considered the last t.A.T.u. video even though Julia's presence is only represented by a photograph and with a stand-in.
In terms of its theme, *Never Forget* is related to the last single, *Snowfalls,* in which Boris wanted to portray the (self-) destruction

---

[231] Jason Lipshutz, *T.A.T.u.Calls It Quits Following Release of Remix Album,* Billboard.com, 4 April 2011.

of the group through the suicide motorcycle crash between Lena and Julia. In the new video the two heroines are dead and Cox shows them lying in a cold mortuary, then a small group of people attend their funeral. The ghost of Lena (kissing Julia's picture one last time) hovers over them, accompanying their last journey to a grassy cemetery where two simple headstones bear their real names and years of birth, beside the date of the death of t.A.T.u. in 2011.

SOLO CAREERS AND REUNION

In the months that follow Lena and Julia devote themselves entirely to their solo careers, avoiding all contact with each other even by phone; as Lena reveals in an interview[232] 'we were tired of t.A.T.u. and tired of each other.' Whenever they're asked[233], both maintain that they have no intention of getting together again, at least for the foreseeable future.

Never Forget doesn't bring much success for Lena, but Dave Audé's remixed version of it reaches the top spot in the Billboard.com chart (Club dance section). Julia misses out on Eurovision 2012 by a hair's breadth, coming second to singer Dima Bilan in the national selection, and in summer that year she releases her single *Didn't Wanna Do It*. Both girls, however, fail to produce an entire solo album, despite repeated announcements particularly from Lena, who has no recording contract and is limited in her efforts to featuring alongside other artists.

But t.A.T.u.'s early successes remain very popular in Europe in spite of the length of time that's elapsed since then and the fact that the group has now broken up. In February 2012 *All the Things She Said* makes a return to the European charts as one of the 200 most downloaded tracks, and on 2nd October something unexpected happens for t.A.T.u. fans, who by this time are resigned to them staying apart. On the tenth anniversary of the album *200 Km/h In The Wrong Lane*, Cherrytree Records, a subsidiary of Interscope/Universal directed by Martin Kierszenbaum who has

---

[232] Marina Ahmedova, *"Никогда не забуду"*, *Russian Reporter*, 24 January 2012.
[233] Igor Cuzovic, *"Plakala sam zbog Jugoslavije"*, *Kurir Serbia*, 15 January 2012.

evidently not forgotten the golden years with Julia and Lena, announces the release of a commemorative edition of t.A.T.u.'s historic first international album, under the banner '10th *Anniversary Edition.*' The LP, officially released on November 12 to commemorate the anniversary of the original release, contains the unreleased track *A Simple Motion* (remember that this was supposed to be on the album *The Best* in 2006) as well as some new remixes. Many people expect Julia and Lena to be involved in some way, but their involvement seems limited to a few sentences about it by each of them on their Facebook pages.

Actually, something is bubbling away on the back burner, but nothing has yet leaked out about it: in the months leading up to the release Julia had admitted she was ready to meet Lena for the first time in two years and discuss with her the possibility of some kind of collaboration, but they all consider Boris to be an insurmountable obstacle to it. So the possibility of any reunion seems fairly remote, even though Sergio Galoyan, who's just released a single by Lena at the beginning of November (*Paradise*) admits on the phone that there's a surprise in the offing.

On November 20 Cherrytree make an official announcement: t.A.T.u. are to reunite for a show on December 11 for the first time in three years, for one of the final evenings of the TV talent show, Vocea Romaniei, in Bucharest, Romania. A few days later, while fans of the group are feverishly awaiting more details, they get another surprise: Lena is leaving Boris to become, to all intents and purposes, an independent singer, and she announces the release of her first solo album funded by her fans. Is this the squaring of the circle? The collaboration between Katina and Rensky seems to have ended by mutual agreement, with Boris now exhausted after two years trying (unsuccessfully) to find a record label to release the album, and Lena prepared to put herself totally out there, entrusting herself to the continued loyalty of her group and the affection of a few thousand fans. From this angle, the reunion with

Julia looks like a particularly apt marketing device now that Boris's veto is removed, which might turn the spotlight back on t.A.T.u., and on herself, both in Russia and possibly internationally too. In the days after the show in Romania Julia and Lena do in fact make guest appearances on many radio and television programmes in Eastern Europe, which has the immediate effect of taking some of the tracks from the commemorative LP temporarily back into the charts in a number of countries, such as Ukraine where *A Simple Motion* reaches no. 26.

Despite the expectations of many of their fans who are encouraged by seeing Lena and Julia hand in hand once again on stage, their collaboration is restricted to just a few performances: a semi-private event on 25th April 2013 at the Kalina Bar in Moscow and another on 27th September at the Stereoplaza in Kiev, Ukraine. Meanwhile, Lena tries to give her solo career new impetus (which stalled again after she split with Boris), dismissing her new manager Tristram Buckley suddenly in March - who brings a lawsuit against her over it - and doing some live performances where she introduces three new songs: *Walking In The Sun, Something I Said* and *Lift Me Up.* The latter song, which later becomes her second solo single, is co-written by Jasmine Ash, Jacques Brautbar and Lena herself, who dedicates it to her fans and supporters. And to this purpose she also collects hundreds of photos sent in by fans in June, with the intention of using them in the video for *Lift Me Up.*

Julia doesn't produce any new singles in 2013, partly because of more problems with her voice, and devotes most of her time to performing in clubs in Russia and promoting the film *Zombie Vacation* in which she stars.

An attempt to establish a better organised and lasting reunion at the beginning of 2014 is a resounding disappointment.

t.A.T.u. are invited to perform at the opening ceremony of the Winter Olympics in Sochi and although it's only the pre-show and will not be broadcast worldwide, the news causes quite a stir internationally for the fact that a group famed for its portrayal of lesbian love is now opening an event that has sparked widespread controversy over recent laws in Russia against so-called 'gay propaganda'[234]. For one week t.A.T.u. are back in the headlines and gossip columns all over the world[235] like they used to be in the golden days, and it seems that this could really be the start of a new era for them. A week after the performance in Sochi t.A.T.u. are unexpectedly included in the Big Love Show in Moscow: the traditional music event held on Valentine's night, sponsored by LoveRadio. As well as the old favourite *Nas Ne Dogonyat* (which actually becomes the Olympic anthem after the song was played out to accompany the Russian athletes in the opening parade), they perform a new song with Russian rapper Ligalize, who co-wrote the song with Mike Tompkins. The producer of the track, which is labelled perhaps prematurely as 't.A.T.u.'s first single in six years' and which has the anything but prophetic title of Love in Every Moment (*Lubov V Kazdom Mgnovenii*), is actually one of the architects of the original project: Elena Kiper.

But fans' enthusiasm for the reunion lasts only a few hours. Four days after the performance in Moscow Lena puts out a video message on her YouTube channel accusing Julia of doing everything she can to take total control of the group's new artistic course, even going as far as to suggest that Lena can be replaced by 'another curly-haired redhead' if she doesn't want to do it herself. Lena seems deeply troubled in her message[236], in which she says she is seriously worried that Volkova might even block her solo career within Russia, and concludes that no kind of

[234] Giulia Zonca, *"t.A.T.u.le furbette delle Olimpiadi. Due finte lesbiche alla cerimonia?"*, *La Stampa*, 31 January 2014.

[235] Sean *Michaels "Pop duo t.A.T.u. reportedly performing at Sochi Winter Olympics"* *The Guardian*, 7 February 2014.

[236] *"Сотрудничество стало абсолютно невозможным: Лена Катина заявила об уходе из t.A.T.u."*, НТВ.ru, 18 February 2014.

collaboration or any dialogue is possible with her (now ex-) partner. A few hours later an iconic black and white image of Lena and Julia with their backs turned appears on the group's official Facebook page, which seems to confirm that the separation this time is final.

CONCLUSIONS

These two girls can touch the soul not just with their music, and not just with people of their own generation.

Boris Rensky, 2007[237]

Like I said at the beginning of this brief history of t.A.T.u., fate propelled them unexpectedly to the heights of the pop music world before they were even sixteen, and then turned its back on them. After their initial international success with *All The Things She Said* and their first album in English, the story of Julia and Lena is subsequently littered with missed opportunities.

The first of these was undoubtedly the fact that they never accomplished a proper world tour. As early as autumn 2002 their association with Interscope had provided t.A.T.u. with the services of a highly professional band, giving them the means to dispense with the clinical practice of lip-synching that characterised their debut, only suitable at best for an adolescent audience and perhaps not good enough even for them; they had the means at their disposal of staging the kind of pop concerts they did eventually produce with the *Dangerous & Moving Tour* in 2006, although by that time it was already too late, and conducted solely within the Russian republics. Extreme delays were brought about by problems with Julia's voice in 2003.

---

[237] Tatu.ru official blog, post by *Insider*, 31 December 2007.

The second and perhaps even more important missed opportunity was with the second album. *Dangerous & Moving* was actually a great album, more sophisticated than the first one, *200 Km/h In The Wrong Lane*, with excellent arrangement and production through their involvement with major organisations like Interscope and Universal, and exactly the kind of thing to take their fans by the hand and lead them into deeper waters as they grew up and developed more mature musical tastes. Unfortunately, this album should have come out much sooner, at the end of 2003 or spring 2004 at the latest, as Universal intended. Not autumn 2005, at which point t.A.T.u.'s international reputation was in tatters, as demonstrated by sales of the album which were way below what was expected and what the album was capable of. The massive delay was almost entirely down to Shapovalov, who probably envisaged t.A.T.u. originally as just a one-hit-wonder, not a proper group. Vanya actually said as much to Julia and Lena in 2003 when he suggested ending it.

The third missed opportunity, although somewhat less significant than the first two, was the Eurovision Song Contest in 2003. t.A.T.u. were the favourites to win; their notoriety and their famous Euro-pop sound would have carried them to first place even if they'd been wearing gags and had sung with their microphones switched off. Yet they managed to ruin even this opportunity, through Julia's ailments to some extent, but mainly because of the nonsensical communication policy with the press and their relationship with the international organisers of the event. A win in Riga would have kept t.A.T.u.'s international press coverage going for several months exactly when they needed it - their blackout period caused by Julia's voice problems. By accepting the nomination, despite the girls' opposition to taking part, Vanja acted with foresight on this occasion, realising it was the only way to keep the group's popularity going for the period during which they were unable to give performances.

There were countless other missed opportunities relating to the concerts cancelled practically everywhere, undermining the credibility of the group and disappointing thousands of fans. And then there's the well-documented 'tatuism' and Julia's whims (according to Boris Rensky), the insistence on holding concerts in large arenas everywhere instead of more modest venues, less productive in terms of revenue but easier to fill, which contributed in no small way to destroying relationships with local organisations - so important for building a solid foundation for t.A.T.u.'s future.

Something that Troy said in reply to a fan on his blog, is pertinent in this respect:

> It was really hard to be in TATU and watch mistake after mistake being made with the way the band was being run & managed. (Troy Maccubbin, 2011)

One last opportunity that was left unexploited, this time for reasons beyond the control of t.A.T.u., was the film *You and I.* We have already seen how a more appropriate date for releasing the film would have increased box office receipts for its producers and pumped vital oxygen into the group which was gasping for breath by this time.

But apparently it was foretold that Julia and Lena should part. It is a miracle they lasted as long as they did, and had almost twelve years together; Lena had already expressed a desire to go solo in 2003, and practically announced it in January 2004. Then it was Julia in 2007, and finally the irremediable crisis of 2008, although the group technically managed to survive until 2011. If that's how it was, Lena says today with great firmness, all the credit should go to Rensky:

> After we split from Vanja Julia and I thought there'd be were dozens of managers and producers queuing up to take t.A.T.u. on, but we were mistaken: there was no queue and no one willing to take the project forward. There was only Boris, who really made an enormous effort and to whom we owe almost everything. (Lena Katina, 2013)

Imagine where Lena and Julia could be today if just one of these missed opportunities had been exploited; it's not easy. Certainly, if the second album had been released at least a year earlier sales figures would have been a lot more interesting for Universal, who would in all probability have retained their contract with them, and the connection with Interscope would have assured t.A.T.u. of a much rosier future.

But these reflections are futile. What fans are left with today is a few dozen songs, some of which are already classics, some memorable videos, thousands of photographs and hours of video footage showing t.A.T.u. all over the world. What Julia and Lena have come out of it with is economic security and a wealth of professional experience, and more importantly, invaluable memories of sharing such a close bond with someone, and a level of success that many international artists will never even come close to.

> It was a huge success all of a sudden. My childhood dream came true. There can be only one regret: That these years pass too quickly, and there's no way to return back. (Julia Volkova, 2012)[238]

---

[238] Bradley Stern, *"10 Years in the wrong lane: an interview with t.A.T.u."*, *MuuMuse*, November 2012.

DISCOGRAPHY

Ya Soshla S Uma
Maxi-CD Single
2000
Neformat

1. "Ya Soshla S Uma (Я сошла с ума)" (Original edit) (S. Galoyan, E. Kiper, V. Polienko) - 3:34
2. "Ya Soshla S Uma (Я сошла с ума)" (DJ Ram Remix) - 4:03
3. "Ya Soshla S Uma (Я сошла с ума)" (Galoyan Slow Remix) - 4:31
4. "Ya Soshla S Uma (Я сошла с ума)" (Galoyan Breakbeat Remix) - 3:38
5. "Ya Soshla S Uma (Я сошла с ума)" (HarDrum Remix) - 4:08

- "Ya Soshla S Uma (Я сошла с ума)" (Music Video)
- "Ya Soshla S Uma (Я сошла с ума)" (HarDrum Remix Video)

200 Po Vstrechnoy*
LP
2001
Neformat

1. "Zachem Ya (Зачем я)" (A. Voitinskiy, A. Vulih, I. Shapovalov, V. Polienko) - 4:07
2. "Ya Soshla s Uma (Я сошла с ума)" (S. Galoyan, E. Kiper, V. Polienko) - 3:30
3. "Nas Ne Dogonyat (Нас не догонят)" (S. Galoyan, E. Kiper, I. Shapovalov, V. Polienko) - 4:38
4. "Doschitay Do Sta (Досчитай до ста)" (A. Voitinskiy, V. Polienko) - 4:37
5. "30 Minut (30 минут) (*Polchasa*)" (S. Galoyan, I. Shapovalov, V. Polienko) - 3:17
6. "Ya Tvoy Vrag (Я твой враг)" (R. Ryabzeb) - 4:16
7. "Ya Tvoya Ne Pervaya (Я твоя не первая) (*Pokazhi Mne Lyubov'*)" (S. Galoyan, V. Polienko) - 4:17
8. "Robot (Робот)" (A. Voitinskiy, V. Polienko) - 3:53
9. "Mal'chik-Gey (Мальчик-гей)" (S. Galoyan, A. Karaseva, V. Stepandsov) - 3:18
10. "Nas Ne Dogonyat (Нас не догонят) (HarDrum Remix)" - 3:50
11. "30 Minut (30 минут) (*Polchasa*) (HarDrum Remix)" - 4:02
12. "Ya Soshla s Uma (Я сошла с ума) (HarDrum Remix)" (S. Galoyan, E. Kiper, V. Polienko) - 4:13 (Hidden Track starts at 5:04 on Tr. 11)

197

200 Po Vstrechnoy - Reissue*
LP
2002
Universal Music Russia

1. "Klouny (Клоуны)" (I. Shapovalov, E. Kuritsin, V. Polienko) - 3:32
2. "30 Minut (30 минут) (*Polchasa*)" - 3:20
3. "Doschitay Do Sta (Досчитай до 100 [ста])" - 4:38
4. "Zachem Ya (Зачем я)" - 4:10
5. "Nas Ne Dogonyat (Нас не догонят)" - 4:39
6. "Ya Tvoya Ne Pervaya (Я твоя не первая) (*Pokazhi Mne Lyubov'*)" - 4:19
7. "Robot (Робот)" - 3:54
8. "Mal'chik-Gey (Мальчик-гей)" - 3:20
9. "Ya Tvoy Vrag (Я твой враг)" - 4:19
10. "Ya Soshla s Uma (Я сошла с ума)" - 3:33
11. "30 Minut (30 минут) (*Polchasa*) (Moscow Grooves Institute Remix)" - 5:58
12. "Mal'chik-Gey (Мальчик-гей) (That Black Remix)" - 5:05

All The Things She Said*
Maxi-CD Single
2002
Interscope Records

1. "All The Things She Said" (S. Galoyan, T. Horn, M. Kierszenbaum, E. Kiper, V. Polienko) (Radio Version) - 3:31
2. "All The Things She Said" (S. Galoyan, T. Horn, M. Kierszenbaum, E. Kiper, V. Polienko) (Extension 119 Club Edit) - 5:16

- "All The Things She Said" (Music Video)
- "Behind The Scenes With Julia & Lena (Part 1)" (Video)

All The Things She Said (Remixes)*
Maxi-CD Single
2002
Interscope Records

1. "All The Things She Said (S. Galoyan, T. Horn, M. Kierszenbaum, E. Kiper, V. Polienko) (Radio Version)" - 3:31
2. "All The Things She Said (S. Galoyan, T. Horn, M. Kierszenbaum, E. Kiper, V. Polienko) (Mark!'s Intellectual Vocal Mix)" - 9:41
3. "All The Things She Said (S. Galoyan, T. Horn, M. Kierszenbaum, E. Kiper, V. Polienko) (Extension 119 Club Edit)" - 5:17
4. "All The Things She Said (S. Galoyan, T. Horn, M. Kierszenbaum, E. Kiper, V. Polienko) (HarDrum Remix)" - 4:08

200 Km/h In The Wrong Lane*
LP - Enhanced
2002
Interscope Records

1. "Not Gonna Get Us" (S. Galoyan, T. Horn, E. Kiper, I. Shapovalov, V. Polienko) - 4:21
2. "All The Things She Said" (S. Galoyan, T. Horn, M. Kierszenbaum, E. Kiper, V. Polienko) - 3:34
3. "Show Me Love" (S. Galoyan, M. Kierszenbaum, V. Polienko) - 4:15
4. "30 Minutes" (S. Galoyan, M. Kierszenbaum, I. Shapovalov, V. Polienko) - 3:18
5. "How Soon Is Now?" (Johnny Marr, Morrissey) - 3:15
6. "Clowns (Can You See Me Now?)" (I. Shapovalov, E. Kuritsin, T. Horn, V. Polienko) - 3:12
7. "Malchik Gay" (S. Galoyan, M. Kierszenbaum, A. Karaseva, V. Stepandsov) - 3:09
8. "Stars" (A. Voitinskiy, M. Kierszenbaum, A. Vulih, I. Shapovalov, V. Polienko) - 4:08
9. "Ya Soshla S Uma (Я сошла с ума)" (S. Galoyan, E. Kiper, V. Polienko) - 3:34
10. "Nas Ne Dogonyat (Нас не догонят)" (S. Galoyan, E. Kiper, I. Shapovalov, V. Polienko) - 4:22
11. "Show Me Love (Extended Version)" - 5:10

- "30 Minutes (Remix)" - 5:52 "Behind The Scenes with Julia and Lena (Part 2)" (Video)
- "All The Things She Said" (Music Video)

Deluxe Edition extras:

CD

13. "Ne Ver', Ne Boisya" (Mars Lasar, Ivan Shapovalov, Valeriy Polienko) - 3:02

DVD

- "Julia + Lena Are t.A.T.u." Documentary
- All The Things She Said (Music Video)
- Not Gonna Get Us (Music Video)
- How Soon Is Now? (Music Video)

Not Gonna Get Us*
Maxi-CD single
2003
Interscope Records

1. "Not Gonna Get Us" (S. Galoyan, T. Horn, E. Kiper, I. Shapovalov, V. Polienko) (Radio Version) - 3:38
2. "Not Gonna Get Us" (S. Galoyan, T. Horn, E. Kiper, I. Shapovalov, V. Polienko) (Dave Audé's Extension 119 Vocal Edit) - 3:54
3. "All The Things She Said" (S. Galoyan, T. Horn, M. Kierszenbaum, E. Kiper, V. Polienko) (DJ Monk's Breaks Mix) - 6:04
4. "All The Things She Said" (S. Galoyan, T. Horn, M. Kierszenbaum, E. Kiper, V. Polienko) (Blackpulke Remix)- 4:13

- " Not Gonna Get Us" (Music Video)

Not Gonna Get Us Remixes*
Maxi-CD single
2003
Interscope Records

1. "Not Gonna Get Us" (S. Galoyan, T. Horn, E. Kiper, I. Shapovalov, V. Polienko) (Dave Aude Extension 119 Club Vocal) - 3:54
2. "Not Gonna Get Us" (S. Galoyan, T. Horn, E. Kiper, I. Shapovalov, V. Polienko) (Richard Morel Pink Noise Vocal Mix) – 8:12
3. "Not Gonna Get Us" (S. Galoyan, T. Horn, E. Kiper, I. Shapovalov, V. Polienko) (Radio Version) – 3:38
4. "All The Things She Said" (S. Galoyan, T. Horn, M. Kierszenbaum, E. Kiper, V. Polienko) (Guena LG & RLS Extended Mix)- 5:38

How Soon Is Now - Germany*
Maxi-CD single
2003
Interscope Records

1. "How Soon Is Now?" (Johnny Marr, Morrissey) - 3:15
2. "Ne Ver, Ne Boisya (Eurovision 2003 Version)" (Mars Lasar, Ivan Shapovalov, Valeriy Polienko) - 3:02
3. "30 Minutes" (S. Galoyan, M. Kierszenbaum, I. Shapovalov, V. Polienko) (Moscow Grooves Institute Remix) - 5:52
4. "Not Gonna Get Us" (S. Galoyan, T. Horn, E. Kiper, I. Shapovalov, V. Polienko) (HarDrum Remix) - 3:50

Remixes*
LP - Compilation
2003
Interscope Records

1. "All the Things She Said" (S. Galoyan, T. Horn, M. Kierszenbaum, E. Kiper, V. Polienko) (DJ Monk's After Skool Special) - 4:15
2. "All the Things She Said" (S. Galoyan, T. Horn, M. Kierszenbaum, E. Kiper, V. Polienko) (Mark!'s Buzzin Mix) - 8:14
3. "All the Things She Said" (S. Galoyan, T. Horn, M. Kierszenbaum, E. Kiper, V. Polienko) (Running And Spinning Remix) - 6:15
4. "All the Things She Said" (S. Galoyan, T. Horn, M. Kierszenbaum, E. Kiper, V. Polienko) (Dave Audé's Extension 119 Club Dub) -8:19

5.   "Not Gonna Get Us" (S. Galoyan, T. Horn, E. Kiper, I. Shapovalov, V. Polienko) (Larry Tee Electroclash Mix) - 6:21
6.   "Not Gonna Get Us" (S. Galoyan, T. Horn, E. Kiper, I. Shapovalov, V. Polienko) (Richard Morel's Pink Noise Vocal Mix) - 8:12
7.   "Not Gonna Get Us" (S. Galoyan, T. Horn, E. Kiper, I. Shapovalov, V. Polienko) (Thick Dick Vocal) - 7:14
8.   "Not Gonna Get Us" (S. Galoyan, T. Horn, E. Kiper, I. Shapovalov, V. Polienko) (D. Audé Remix - Velvet Dub Aka Big Dub Mix) - 7:16
9.   "30 Minutes" (S. Galoyan, M. Kierszenbaum, I. Shapovalov, V. Polienko) (Dave Audé's Extension 119 Club Vocal) - 7:59

• "Not Gonna Get Us" (Remix Video)

Deluxe Edition extras:

CD 1

10.   Простые Движения (Prostye Dvizheniya) - 3:58
11.   Не Верь, Не Бойся (Ne Ver', Ne Boisya) – 3:05

CD 2

1.   Я Сошла С Ума (Ya Soshla S Uma) (HarDrum Remix)
2.   All The Things She Said (HarDrum Remix)
3.   Нас Не Догонят (Nas Ne Dogonyat) (HarDrum Remix)
4.   30 Минут (30 Minut) (HarDrum Remix)
5.   30 Минут (30 Minut) (Naked Mix)
6.   30 Минут (30 Minut) (Raga Mix)
7.   Мальчик-Гей (Mal'chik-Gey) (Fanky Mix)
8.   All The Things She Said (Extension 119 Club Edit)
9.   All The Things She Said (DJ Monk's Breaks Mix)

DVD

• Я Сошла С Ума (Ya Soshla S Uma)
• Я Сошла С Ума (Ya Soshla S Uma) (HarDrum Remix)
• Нас Не Догонят (Nas Ne Dogonyat)
• 30 Минут (30 Minut)
• Простые Движения (Prostye Dvizheniya)
• All The Things She Said
• All The Things She Said (Extension 119 Club Edit)
• Not Gonna Get Us
• Not Gonna Get Us (Dave Audé Velvet Dub)
• 30 Minutes
• How Soon Is Now?
• Не Верь, Не Бойся (Ne Ver', Ne Boisya) (Live At МузTv Awards 2003)
• Нас Не Догонят (Nas Ne Dogonyat) (Live At МузTv Awards 2003)

Lyudi Invalidy*
LP
2005
Universal Music Russia

1. "Lyudi Invalidy (Intro) (Люди Инвалиды)" (I. Shapovalov) - 0:49
2. "Novaya Model' (Новая Модель)" (S. Galoyan, V. Polienko) - 4:12
3. "Obez'yanka Nol' (Обезьянка Ноль)" (V. Adarichev, A. Pokutni, V. Polienko) - 4:25
4. "Loves Me Not" (E. Buller, A. Kubiszewski) - 3:14
5. "Kosmos (Космос)" (S. Galoyan, V. Polienko) - 4:12
6. "Ty Soglasna? (Ты Согласна?)" (V. Adarichev, A. Pokutni, V. Polienko) - 3:10
7. "Nich'ya (Ничья)" (Nekkermann, V. Polienko) - 3:02
8. "Vsya Moya Lyubov' (Вся Моя Любовь)" (Nekkermann, V. Polienko) - 5:52
9. "All About Us" (J. Alexander, B. Steinberg, L. Origliasso, J. Origliasso) - 3:00
10. "Chto Ne Hvatayet (Что Не Хватает)" (I. Demyan) - 4:25
11. "Lyudi Invalidy (Люди Инвалиды)" (I. Shapovalov, V. Polienko) - 4:35

All About Us*
Maxi-CD single
2005
Interscope Records

1. "All About Us" (J. Alexander, B. Steinberg, L. Origliasso, J. Origliasso) (Single Version) - 3:05
2. "Divine" (Alias, Martin Kierszenbaum) (Non-LP Long Version) - 3:17
3. "All About Us" (J. Alexander, B. Steinberg, L. Origliasso, J. Origliasso) (Stephane K Mix Radio Edit) - 4:01

• "All about Us" (Explicit Music Video) – 3:26

Dangerous And Moving*
LP
2005
Interscope Records

1. "Dangerous and Moving (Intro)" (I. Shapovalov) - 0:49
2. "All About Us" (J. Alexander, B. Steinberg, L. Origliasso, J. Origliasso) - 3:00
3. "Cosmos (Outer Space)" (S. Galoyan, M. Kierszenbaum, L. Alexandrovski, V. Polienko) - 4:11
4. "Loves Me Not" (E. Buller, A. Kubiszewski) - 2:55
5. "Friend or Foe" (M. Kierszenbaum, D. Stewart) - 3:08
6. "Gomenasai" (M. Kierszenbaum) - 3:42
7. "Craving (I Only Want What I Can't Have)" (L. Lindley-Jones) - 3:50
8. "Sacrifice" (S. Galoyan, M. Kierszenbaum) - 3:09
9. "We Shout" (Nekkermann, M. Kierszenbaum, L. Alexandrovski, V. Polienko) - 3:02
10. "Perfect Enemy" (S. Galoyan, M. Kierszenbaum, T.A. Music, V. Polienko) - 4:12

11. "Obezyanka Nol (Обезьянка Ноль)" (V. Adarichev, A. Pokutni, V. Polienko) - 4:25
12. "Dangerous and Moving" (I. Shapovalov, M. Kierszenbaum, L. Alexandrovski, T.A. Music, V. Polienko) - 4:35
13. "Vsya Moya Lyubov' (Вся Моя Любовь)" (S. Galoyan, M. Kierszenbaum, V. Polienko) - 5:50
14. "Lyudi Invalidy (Люди Инвалиды)" (I. Shapovalov) - 4:35

Deluxe Edition extras:

DVD (Europe)

- The Making Of "All About Us" Music Video
- All About Us (Music Video)

All About Us Part. 2: The Remixes
Maxi-CD single
2005
Interscope Records

1. "All About Us" (J. Alexander, B. Steinberg, L. Origliasso, J. Origliasso) (Glam As You Mix By Guéna LG) – 6:25
2. "All About Us" (J. Alexander, B. Steinberg, L. Origliasso, J. Origliasso) (Sunset in Ibiza Mix By Guéna LG) – 8:26
3. "All About Us" (J. Alexander, B. Steinberg, L. Origliasso, J. Origliasso) (Dave Audé Big Room Vocal) – 7:59
4. "All About Us" (J. Alexander, B. Steinberg, L. Origliasso, J. Origliasso) (The Lovemakers Mix) – 4:51
5. "All About Us" (J. Alexander, B. Steinberg, L. Origliasso, J. Origliasso) (Stephane K Extended Mix – 6:23

Friend Or Foe*
Maxi-CD Single
2005
Interscope Records

1. "Friend or Foe" (M. Kierszenbaum, D. Stewart) (Radio Edit) - 3:07
2. "All About Us" (J. Alexander, B. Steinberg, L. Origliasso, J. Origliasso) (Sunset In Ibiza Mix) - 4:24
3. "Friend or Foe" (M. Kierszenbaum, D. Stewart) (Morel's Pink Noise Mix) - 6:54

- "Friend or Foe" (Music Video)

Friend Or Foe Part. 2
Maxi-CD Single
2005
Interscope Records

1. "Friend or Foe" (M. Kierszenbaum, D. Stewart) (Glam As You Mix By Guéna LG) – 7:15
2. "Friend or Foe" (M. Kierszenbaum, D. Stewart) (Lenny Bertoldo Club Mix) – 7:31
3. "Friend or Foe" (M. Kierszenbaum, D. Stewart) (L.E.X. Massive Dub) – 7:54
4. "Friend or Foe" (M. Kierszenbaum, D. Stewart) (Morel's Pink Noise Mix) - 6:53
5. "Friend or Foe" (M. Kierszenbaum, D. Stewart) (Lenny Bertoldo Dub) – 8:19

Gomenasai*
Maxi-CD Single
2006
Interscope Records

1. "Gomenasai" (M. Kierszenbaum) - 3:44
2. "Cosmos (Outer Space)" (S. Galoyan, M. Kierszenbaum, L. Alexandrovski, V. Polienko) (She Wants Revenge Remix) - 5:39
3. "Craving (I Only Want What I Can't Have)" (L. Lindley-Jones) (Bollywood Mix) - 4:14

• "Gomenasai" (Music Video)

The Best*
LP - Compilation
2006
Interscope Records

1. "All About Us" (J. Alexander, B. Steinberg, L. Origliasso, J. Origliasso) - 3:01
2. "All The Things She Said" (S. Galoyan, T. Horn, M. Kierszenbaum, E. Kiper, V. Polienko) - 3:34
3. "Not Gonna Get Us" (S. Galoyan, T. Horn, E. Kiper, I. Shapovalov, V. Polienko) - 4:20
4. "How Soon Is Now?" (Johnny Marr, Morrissey) - 3:14
5. "Loves Me Not" (E. Buller, A. Kubiszewski) - 2:54
6. "Friend or Foe" (M. Kierszenbaum, D. Stewart) (Radio Version) - 3:06
7. "Gomenasai" (M. Kierszenbaum) - 3:42
8. "Null & Void" (M. Kierszenbaum, V. Polienko, V. Adarichec, A. Pokutni) - 4:25
9. "Cosmos (Outer Space)" (S. Galoyan, M. Kierszenbaum, L. Alexandrovski, V. Polienko) (She Wants Revenge Remix) - 5:36
10. "Show Me Love" (S. Galoyan, M. Kierszenbaum, V. Polienko) (Radio Version) - 3:49
11. "Craving (I Only Want What I Can't Have)" (L. Lindley-Jones) (Bollywood Mix) - 4:08
12. "Ne Ver, Ne Boisya" (Mars Lasar, Ivan Shapovalov, Valeriy Polienko) - 3:02
13. "30 Minutes" (S. Galoyan, M. Kierszenbaum, I. Shapovalov, V. Polienko) - 3:16
14. "Divine" (Alias, Martin Kierszenbaum) (Extended Version) - 3:17
15. "Perfect Enemy" (S. Galoyan, M. Kierszenbaum, T.A. Music, V. Polienko) - 4:09

16. "All The Things She Said" (S. Galoyan, T. Horn, M. Kierszenbaum, E. Kiper, V. Polienko) (Dave Audé Remix Edit) - 5:15
17. "Lyudi Invalidy" (I. Shapovalov) (Russian Version Remix) - 3:22
18. "Loves Me Not" (E. Buller, A. Kubiszewski) (Glam As You Mix Radio Edit) - 3:11
19. "Nas Ne Dogonyat (Нас не догонят)" (S. Galoyan, E. Kiper, I. Shapovalov, V. Polienko) - 4:21
20. "Ya Soshla S Uma (Я сошла с ума)" (S. Galoyan, E. Kiper, V. Polienko) - 3:34

Deluxe Edition extras:

DVD

- Glam As You Concert (Live In France)
- Gomenasai
- Gomenasai (Animated Version)
- How Soon Is Now?
- Lyudi Invalidy
- All About Us (Explicit Version)
- All About Us (Edited Version)
- Friend Or Foe
- All The Things She Said (Remix)
- Not Gonna Get Us (Remix)
- All About Us (Remix)
- Friend Or Foe (Remix)
- All About Us - The Making Of
- Friend Or Foe - The Making Of With Sting
- Gomenasai - The Making Of The Song With Richard Carpenter
- T.V. Spots (Japan)
- T.V. Spots (Germany)
- T.V. Spots (France)
- T.V. Spots (Taiwan)
- T.V. Spots (United Kingdom)
- T.V. Spots (Russia)

Beliy Plaschik - Hyperion Plate
Maxi-CD Single + DVD
2008
T.A. Music

1. "Beliy Plaschik (Белый Плащик)" (V. Kilar, L. Alexandrovski, M. Maxakova, T.A. Music) - 3:16
2. "White Robe" (V. Kilar, L. Alexandrovski, M. Maxakova, T.A. Music) - 3:16
3. "Beliy Plaschik (Белый Плащик)" (V. Kilar, L. Alexandrovski, M. Maxakova, T.A. Music) (Plant of Nothing Remix) - 4:02
4. "Beliy Plaschik (Белый Плащик)" (V. Kilar, L. Alexandrovski, M. Maxakova, T.A. Music) (No Mercy Remix) - 5:38
5. "Beliy Plaschik (Белый Плащик)" (V. Kilar, L. Alexandrovski, M. Maxakova, T.A. Music) (Marsiano Remix) - 4:48
6. "Beliy Plaschik (Белый Плащик)" (V. Kilar, L. Alexandrovski, M. Maxakova, T.A. Music) (House of Robots Remix) - 6:23

7. "Beliy Plaschik (Белый Плащик)" (V. Kilar, L. Alexandrovski, M. Maxakova, T.A. Music) (Astero Remix) - 5:23
8. "220" (V. Polienko, L. Alexandrovski) - 3:10

DVD

1. Beliy Plaschik Video Cut TV
2. Beliy Plaschik Uncensored
3. Making The Video "Beliy Plaschik"

Vesyolye Ulybki
LP
2008
T.A. Music

1. "Intro" (V. Kilar) - 3:09
2. "Beliy Plaschik (Белый Плащик)" (V. Kilar, M. Maxakova, T.A. Music) - 3:14
3. "You And I" (E. Buller, A. Kubiszewski) - 3:16
4. "Snegopady (Снегопады)" (Slowman, K. Salem, T.A. Music) - 3:15
5. "220" (V. Polienko. L. Alexandrovski) - 3:07
6. "Marsianskie Glaza (Марсианские Глаза)" (S. Galoyan, T.A. Music) - 3:10
7. "Chelovechki (Человечки)" (Slowman, T.A. Music) - 3:27
8. "Vesyolye Ulybki (Весёлые Улыбки)" (E. Matveidzev) - 2:04
9. "Running Blind" (J. Schramm, L. Reinatz, C. Behrens, Sven Martin, R. Schwenger, L. Dissing) - 3:39
10. "Fly on the Wall" (J. Alexander, B. Steinberg) - 3:59
11. "Vremya Luny (Время Луны)" (V. Kilar, T.A. Music) - 3:23
12. "Ne Zhaley (Не Жалей)" (V. Kilar, T.A. Music) - 3:06

Waste Management*
LP
2009
T.A. Music

1. "White Robe" (V. Kilar, L. Alexandrovski, M. Maxakova, T.A. Music) - 3:09
2. "You and I" (E. Buller, A. Kubiszewski) - 4:27
3. "Sparks" (V. Polienko, L. Alexandrovski) - 3:30
4. "Snowfalls" (Slowman, L. Alexandrovski, K. Salem, T.A. Music) - 4:12
5. "Marsianskie Glaza" (Марсианские Глаза) (Martian Eyes)" (S. Galoyan, T.A. Music) - 4:10
6. "Little People" (Slowman, L. Alexandrovski, T.A. Music) - 4:19
7. "Waste Management" (E. Matveidzev) - 2:49
8. "Running Blind" (J. Schramm, L. Reinatz, C. Behrens, S. Martin, R. Schwenger, L. Dissing) - 4:41
9. "Fly on the Wall" (J. Alexander, B. Steinberg) - 5:09
10. "Time of the Moon" (V. Kilar, L. Alexandrovski, T.A. Music) - 4:36
11. "Don't Regret" (V. Kilar, L. Alexandrovski, T.A. Music) - 4:26
12. "Clock-Work" - 0:11

13. "Beliy Plaschik" (V. Kilar, M. Maxakova, T.A. Music) (Fly_Dream Remix) - 5:32
14. "Running Blind" (J. Schramm, L. Reinatz, C. Behrens, Sven Martin, R. Schwenger, L. Dissing) (Transformer Remix)" - 3:51
15. "Ne Zhaley" (V. Kilar, T.A. Music) (Sniper Remix)" - 4:57

Waste Management Remixes*

Maxi-CD double - digital only
2011
T.A. Music

CD 1

1. Time of the Moon (Jamcat Jr. Remix) - 4:57
2. Little People (Jamcat Jr. Remix) - 4:21
3. Time of the Moon (Zo-Ya And Weed Remix) - 4:29
4. Ne Zhaley (Korobki-Mix) (Twenty Four Remix) - 3:10
5. Time of the Moon (Dub Remix) - 4:02
6. Don't Regret (Schecter Remix) - 3:48
7. Time of the Moon (Baraka Remix) - 5:25
8. Time of the Moon (Alex Theory & Gaudi Remix) - 5:58

CD 2

1. Ne Zhaley (Muravski Remix) - 3:34
2. White Robe (Anair Remix) - 3:41
3. Time of the Moon (Magø's Lunar Lander Remix) - 7:25
4. White Robe (Shinigami's Kitchen Remix) - 8:57
5. Chelovechki (Distorted Remix) - 4:19
6. Don't Regret (Adir Remix) - 6:23
7. Time of the Moon (Aimoon Psy-Trance Remix) - 8:54
8. Time of the Moon, Beliy Plashik & Ne Zhaley (Chattanooga Ska Orchestra) - 3:46

200 Km/h In The Wrong Lane – 10th Anniversary Edition*

LP – Enhanced - Reissue
2012
Cherrytree Records

1. "A Simple Motion" (M. Lasar, I. Shapovalov, M. Kierszenbaum, V. Polienko) - 2:48
2. "Not Gonna Get Us" (S. Galoyan, T. Horn, E. Kiper, I. Shapovalov, V. Polienko) - 4:21
3. "All The Things She Said" (S. Galoyan, T. Horn, M. Kierszenbaum, E. Kiper, V. Polienko) - 3:34
4. "Show Me Love" (S. Galoyan, M. Kierszenbaum, V. Polienko) - 4:15
5. "30 Minutes" (S. Galoyan, M. Kierszenbaum, I. Shapovalov, V. Polienko) - 3:18
6. "How Soon Is Now?" (Johnny Marr, Morrissey) - 3:15
7. "Clowns (Can You See Me Now?)" (I. Shapovalov, E. Kuritsin, T. Horn, V. Polienko) - 3:12
8. "Malchik Gay" (S. Galoyan, M. Kierszenbaum, A. Karaseva, V. Stepandsov) - 3:09

9.   "Stars" (A. Voitinskiy, M. Kierszenbaum, A. Vulih, I. Shapovalov, V. Polienko) - 4:08
10.   "Ya Soshla S Uma" (S. Galoyan, E. Kiper, V. Polienko) - 3:34
11.   "Nas Ne Dogonyat" (S. Galoyan, E. Kiper, I. Shapovalov, V. Polienko) - 4:22
12.   "Show Me Love (Extended Version)" - 5:10
13.   "30 Minutes (Remix)" - 5:52
14.   "All The Things She Said" (Fernando Garibay Remix) - 4:01
15.   "Show Me Love" (Fabricated Remix) - 4:04

VIDEO RELEASES

Т.А.Т.У. - А.Н.А.Т.О.М.И.Я.
DVD (documentary)
2003
CP Digital

- Документальный Фильм (director: Vitaly Mansky)

t.A.T.u. - Screaming For More
DVD (music video)
2004
Interscope Records

- All The Things She Said
- Я Сошла С Ума
- All The Things She Said (Remix)
- Not Gonna Get Us
- Нас Не Догонят
- Not Gonna Get Us (Remix)
- 30 Minutes
- How Soon Is Now?
- Behind The Scenes With Julia And Lena (Part 1)
- Behind The Scenes With Julia And Lena (Part 2)
- Behind The Scenes With Julia And Lena (Part 3)
- MTV Europe Music Awards Countdown Performance
- Not Gonna Get Us (Rehearsal)
- Photo Gallery
- Q&A With Julia And Lena

t.A.T.u. - .TRUTH. - Live in St. Petersburg
DVD (music video)
2007
Neformat

1. Intro
2. Lyudi Invalidy
3. All About Us
4. Loves Me Not
5. Sacrifice
6. Nich'ya
7. Friend Or Foe
8. Obez'yanka-Nol'
9. Gomenasai
10. Show Me Love
11. How Soon Is Now?
12. Nas Ne Dogonyat
13. Ne Ver', Ne Boisya, Ne Prosi
14. Ya Soshla S Uma

* Different versions have been released

Made in the USA
Monee, IL
29 December 2020

55892256R00121